Adventurers for God

ADVENTURERS

FOR GOD

by

CLARENCE W. HALL

HARPER & ROW, PUBLISHERS

New York, Evanston, and London

Grateful acknowledgment is made to The Reader's
Digest Association, Inc., for permission to use the following articles, which originally appeared in some-
what different form in *The Reader's Digest:*

The Man Who Conquered Devil's Island, copyright
1947 by The Reader's Digest Association, Inc. *The
Man Who Founded A People* (The Gospel of The
Plow); *Unconquerable Kagawa* (Servant of the Poor):
copyright 1951 by The Reader's Digest Association,
Inc. *He Brought My People Back to Life* (Bolivia's
Most Unforgettable Character); *God's Angry Man*
(One Man Against 'Apartheid'); *Medicine Man on
The Amazon; Through Gates of Splendor:* copyright
© 1956 by The Reader's Digest Association, Inc. *The
White Man Comes to Shangri-La* (The Valley that
Time Forgot); *He's Given Sight to 100,000* (He Gave
Sight to 100,000); *Skipper of The 'Morning Star';
Isle of Hope in Hong Kong* (Chinese Refugees' Best
Friend): copyright © 1957 by The Reader's Digest
Association, Inc. *Two Thousand Tongues to Go,* copy-
right © 1958 by The Reader's Digest Association, Inc.

PHOTOGRAPHS: page 68, top by International News
Photos, bottom by The Salvation Army; pages 135–
138, 140 by Robert Halmi; page 206, top by Wide
World Photos, bottom by Religious News Service;
page 240 by Nate Saint, copyright © 1956 by Sam
Saint, Attorney-in-Fact

C-N

*The Library of Congress catalog entry for
this book appears at the end of the text.*

To all those thousands
of brave and gallant men and women
who have left the comforts and safety of home
to respond with high-beating hearts
to the Divine command:
"Go ye into all the world . . . to every creature!"

Contents

Photographs appear on pages 33–34, 67–68,
133–140, 205–206, 239–240

Acknowledgments

All stories contained in this book were condensed in various issues of *The Reader's Digest* between March 1947 and the present. For permission to print them herein, in their original longer form and with up-to-date material added, the author is indebted to DeWitt Wallace and Lila Acheson Wallace, founders and co-editors of *The Reader's Digest*, without whose unfailing encouragement, editorial stimulation, and abiding interest in Christian missions these stories would never have been written.

"Through Gates of Splendor," written by the author from his own on-the-spot research, supplemented by material supplied by Abe C. Van Der Puy, was first used as a book-length feature in *The Reader's Digest* (August 1956). Later, a book by Elisabeth Elliot, using the same title with the magazine's permission, was published by Harper & Brothers.

"The Gospel of the Plow," which originally appeared under the title "The Man Who Founded a People," was written in collaboration with Dr. Liston Pope, Dean of the Divinity School, Yale University.

Certain portions of the Introduction are taken from the author's own text in *Protestant Panorama*, published in 1951 by Farrar, Strauss & Young.

Acknowledgment is made to the following published works which served as helpful background material in the preparation of the author's original articles: *Naught For Your Comfort*, by Trevor Huddleston (Doubleday); *Kagawa*, by William Axling (Harper); *The Lady Was A Skipper*, by Maribelle Cormack (Hill & Wang); *Devil's Island*, by Charles Péan (Hodder & Stoughton); *The Omi Brotherhood in Nippon*, by William Merrell Vories (Omi Brotherhood Publishing Department).

The author also gratefully acknowledges the invaluable assistance given him by the devoted staffs of the various denominational and interdenominational mission boards in opening their files, responding to endless questions for information, and checking the stories for accuracy before they were put into print.

Introduction

Of all the qualities with which mankind is endowed, none excites in us deeper admiration than *courage*. Especially when that courage is completely selfless, dedicated to a cause higher than one's own search for personal happiness or gain.

The stories comprising this book are dramatic examples of that kind of courage. They were gathered through years of roving the remote corners of earth, on behalf of *The Reader's Digest,* as part of that magazine's never-ending hunt for article subjects whose exploits on behalf of their fellows lift us out of ourselves and serve to remind us that we too can make our lives sublime.

That all the stories are of Christian missionaries is not accidental. As the author has stated elsewhere, "Of all the breeds of brave and gallant men and women, Christian missionaries are to me the most heroic—and the most unaware of their heroism." Because they are so "unaware," and usually so completely disinterested in publicity, their stories too infrequently get told.

Until quite recently, it must be admitted, the popular conception of the missionary, even among people who should know better, was a caricature. To those who had not observed these "adventurers for God" at close range, the missionary was often regarded, when he was thought of at all, as a dedicated but rather dull soul who hustled off to some

far region, at the beck of what he conceived to be the voice
of God but was more likely the urgings of his own malad-
justments, to take his frustrations to a people naïve and un-
inhibited, forcing their splendid bodies into Mother Hubbards and their minds into theological strait-jackets.

But that immature judgment of missionaries has recently
undergone some sharp revision. We are belatedly coming to
see that, as a group, few others have done as much to bring
our topsy-turvy world back on balance, to scatter abroad the
tremendous boons of our democratic way of life, to impress
upon the world our fundamental beliefs in the basic dignity
of all people and their rights to education, modern medical
science, and a chance at a better life for all men.

No one volume, nor a dozen volumes, could hope to cover
the wide range of activity by missionaries around the world.
The stories in this book are merely representative of the broad
sweep of the Christian missions enterprise.

Geographically, their settings are the remoter areas of the
missionary frontier—such as the shut-in Shangri-la of Dutch
New Guinea's mysterious interior; the exotic and scattered
islands of Micronesia in the South and Central Pacific; the
wild North-West Frontier between Pakistan and Afghanistan;
the tragic Devil's Island penal colony in French Guiana; the
brooding reaches of the unbelievably vast Amazon River; the
turbulent veldts and crowded cities of Africa; the tangled
jungles of Ecuador and Peru.

Denominationally, they represent both the larger and
smaller church groupings: Methodist and Baptist, Presbyterian and Congregational, Episcopalian and Anglican, Seventh Day Adventist and Christian and Missionary Alliance;
Salvation Army and Quakers. In their work, the subjects'

denominational affiliation is not important. They are both laymen and members of the ordained ministry; that distinction too is unimportant.

Vocationally, these missionaries are "specialists" in the finest sense of the word—and as such are indicative of the widened field of modern missions which today have room for trained people of almost every kind of talent or interest. They are skilled doctors and surgeons, educators and linguists, agriculturalists and anthropologists, architects and business administrators, social scientists and aircraft pilots, technicians and navigators of sea and air.

These, like the thousands of other present-day missionaries they represent, are inheritors of a great tradition, contributors to a mighty record of achievement—a record still only half appreciated and but slightly understood by the world to which they have given so much.

From Britain and America, during the past century and a half, has flowed a thrilling tide of men and women into every non-Christian land, eager to cast their light into superstition's darkness, eager to burn themselves out for Christ.

William Carey heard the far bugles calling while at his cobbler's bench in England, and he closed his shop door forever that he might open the Gospel door to India. David Livingston heard the bugles while tending a spinning jenny; they pulled him to his feet and projected him into the depths of darkest Africa. Robert Morrison heard them while peering at a map of the Orient in his study, and was immediately off to traipse the China hinterland and bring a Christian literature to a million peasants. Adoniram Judson heard them while reading a sermon entitled "The Star of the East," and he soon was burning up a hundred Burma roads with the Gospel torch. John G. Paton heard them while roving the pleasant pastures of his native Scottish highlands, and promptly set sail for the turbulent tropics and the New Hebrides.

These are but five of a number that is legion. You can call the roll of the intrepid pioneers for hours and never exhaust the list. Some lighted out for the distant horizons with only the Bible under their arms and a call to preach in their hearts; some with medical kits and lancets in hand; some with tools over their shoulders and bags of improved seeds in their pockets; some with degrees in pedagogy or medicine or agriculture or divinity; some with nothing save a spirit burning to "further the Gospel" merely by living with and humbly serving the people. But whyever and wherever they went, they left footprints as long as the stride of God.

Americans more than any other people, and out of all proportion to their numerical strength, have been missionary-minded. That mission-mindedness is part and parcel of their pioneering heritage. The American takes to the frontier, wherever it is, with the habitual drift of a man gravitating to his natural environment. It was the missionary impulse, in large part, that brought the colonists to America in the first place. Both the 1606 and 1609 Virginia charters made plain that one of the chief reasons for settling these shores was the propagation of the Christian faith. That impulse put missionaries in the van of every wagon train off to the westward-moving frontiers, sent them out to meet immigrants, induced them to build churches and schools in immigrant settlements, in big cities and on prairies, in mining towns and lumber camps. For a century and a half, they did not go abroad; their focus was held to the new continent. There was plenty to keep them busy.

It was early in the nineteenth century that American Protestants began to focus their eyes on the far frontiers. While still hurling the tentacles of their faith into every area of American life in need of evangelization, they began reaching out to other lands.

Out they went—to India and Africa, whose immensely rich resources had for centuries tempted foreign plunderers . . . out to lands where the bodies of animals were sacred and men's bodies cheap, where gods were wood and stone, and where misery rode the back and poverty ached in the stomach and hopelessness cried in the heart . . . out to China and Burma and Malaya and the islands of the sea . . . out to the outcaste, the untouchable, the diseased, the blighted. Almost every local church formed its missionary society. Pennies and dimes and dollars began dropping into missionary boxes, clothing and food and books into missionary barrels. Denominational leaders got out their big maps, began to plan world strategy.

Out they went and out they continued to go—right up to the eve of Pearl Harbor. World War II temporarily halted the march, but it brought to blazing light what had been happening in the world's far corners where those immigrants for Christ had gone. American GI's, fanning out all over the world, found some amazing Christians in some amazing places. Back from the war fronts, they sent letters to loved ones telling tales that seemed tall even to supporters of foreign missions. Their lives had been saved by mission-converted ex-cannibals. Their broken and fever-ridden bodies had been transported over the Owen Stanley ranges by "fuzzy-wuzzy" stretcher-bearers with "a look on their faces that makes you think that Christ was black." They had been fished out of the sea, spirited to safety, nursed to health and returned to their comrades by natives who couldn't speak their language but could sing their hymn tunes. Following the blazing path of war, members of the U. S. armed forces came upon Christian communities distinguished by a character of life sharply contrasting with the life around them, met everywhere Bible-carryng and hymn-singing Christians of varied hues where atlases and military intelligence had indicated only savages.

The GI's ran into men of the stature of Albert Schweitzer, one of the towering figures of our time, or any time, a man of tremendously varied talents, content to lose himself in the lives of Africa's black men. They saw men like Sam Higginbottam, who has brought to India his immense achievements in Christian agriculture, and Emory Alvord who in thirty years had changed the face of Southern Rhodesia by the application of his "Gospel of the Plow." They came upon the monuments of Christian healing left by great medical missionaries like Gordon Seagrave, "Burma Surgeon," whose triumphs over disease were such as to make Hippocrates rise from his Grecian grave and applaud. They followed hard upon the trail of men like globe-girdling Frank Laubach who, with his "Each one teach one" program, is generalissimo in the world crusade to stamp out illiteracy among the countless millions on this planet who can neither read nor write—nor, therefore, vote.

The revelation was not alone to servicemen. Franklin D. Roosevelt wrote before his death: "Since becoming President, I have come to know that the finest type of Americans we

have abroad are the missionaries of the Cross. I am hu-
miliated that I am just finding out at this late day the work
of foreign missions and the nobility of the missionary."
Wendell Willkie went junketing around the earth during
the war, and came back to tell of the great "reservoir of good
will" America has in foreign lands, thanks in large part to
missionary enterprise.

By no means the least contribution made by foreign missions is the large part they have played in making Americans global-minded, preparing them for the day, now come,
when this nation would be the free world's leader and its
hope. We tend to forget that, if indeed we ever fully realized
it. As Kenneth Scott Latourette has pointed out, "Even
those most active in the world-wide missionary enterprise are
frequently unaware of how deeply it has molded the American outlook on the world."

During the many decades when millions of American
church members were making their gifts to "the mission half
of the church envelope," listening to addresses by missionaries on furlough, reading of mission projects through church
periodicals, studying missions in church schools, something
pretty important was happening to the American mind. It
was being keyed to the fact that peoples beyond the seas
and beyond our ken were important. More, they have taught
Americans to think *brotherly*—to think about the world's
peoples in a way that had nothing to do with commercial or
political exploitation.

What this has meant, and will mean in the future, nobody
can possibly assess. But one would be both unfair and un-
realistic if, in auditing the reasons for America's growth from
fierce isolationism into world responsibility, he did not ring

with red pencil those long years when Christians have been preaching the infinite worth of man, irrespective of color or race, and when Americans by the millions have been acquiring a universal sympathy, a universal conscience, through their interest in and support of world-wide missions.

And, mind you, this mighty "foreign aid" program is now, and always has been, carried along with no support from the government, no draft upon the taxpayer's pocketbook. By contrast with the billions of government money poured into underdeveloped countries, the funds that Christians have had to work with are peanuts. Yet compare the results! Miserly the pennies that have been put into the missions enterprise, you say? You are right, of course. We should have poured in millions, billions. But what miracles have been wrought all across the world by even the pennies!

Another accomplishment definitely traceable to the missionary enterprise—one that is vital to Christianity's future in the world—is this: it has taught Christians everywhere the meaning of that jaw-breaking word "ecumenicity." Especially has it been taught where the importance of Christian brotherhood and co-operation is needed the worst: among America's great proliferation of religious bodies. Workers out on the world's far-flung fringes, in a sort of reverse missionary movement, have helped "Christianize" their home churches.

No one traveling to far parts and witnessing at first hand the operations of various mission bodies can fail to be struck by the spirit of co-operation and unity that exists among them. The farther you get out onto the frontier, the more Christian brotherhood you find among groups of even the most diverse doctrinal differences. Dog-eat-dog denominationalism might be tolerated, though deplored, on the home front. But out on the mission field it is fatal to both the eater and the eaten. While "competition" among missionary groups has not been banished entirely, one sees far less of it abroad than at home.

It was at a missionary conference at Edinburgh in 1910 that the spirit of ecumenicity, long practiced by experienced missionaries in the field, was finally recognized as a high goal for churches at home as well as abroad. The challenge was first thrown out by Episcopal Bishop Charles H. Brent who declared, "The world is too strong for a divided Church!" Since then the strides toward unified planning and co-operation, particularly among Protestant churches, has been impressive. Christians everywhere today are singing with new understanding,

> In Christ there is no East or West,
> In Him no South or North,
> But one great Fellowship of Love
> Throughout the whole wide earth!

For that—and a great deal else—you can thank the foreign missions program.

To a broader understanding of that program, and of the kind of people who make it dynamic and inspiring, this baker's dozen of stories is sincerely dedicated.

Adventurers for God

I

The Valley That Time Forgot

Christian missionaries, I confess, fascinate me. Of all the breeds of brave and gallant men, they are to me the most heroic—and the most unaware of their heroism. Thus when, in 1956, I heard that a small contingent under the ægis of the Christian and Missionary Alliance had quietly gone into the forbidding interior of Dutch New Guinea, to seek one of the world's most recently discovered tribes, I knew I had to follow them.

On a small airstrip at Sentani Lake, outside Hollandia, New Guinea, I found Dave Steiger. He was changing the spark plugs of a single-engine Piper Pacer, with which he services the "supply line" to remote mission stations.

Dave regarded me doubtfully. To him it was incredible that anyone would fly halfway around the world, then insist upon penetrating into the unexplored fastnesses, just to observe men of God going about their job. He scanned the sky, then shrugged. "Weather's apt to close in over the ranges. But I'll chance it if you will."

Loading emergency supplies, we took off, flew for an hour over impenetrable jungle and swamps, then rose sharply toward an 8000-foot pass into the Snow Mountains. These jagged, towering peaks, some of them rising to 16,000 feet, have isolated the interior for centuries. As we approached them, fog swept in suddenly, blocking out landmarks, closing in behind us. For another hour we floundered about, first trying to get above the clouds, then beneath them.

Finally, through a temporarily clear space in the fog, we sighted a river far below. Dave spiraled down, got under the ceiling and followed the river tumbling through deep gorges. And suddenly our goal, the Grand Valley of the Baliem River —called "Shangri-la" by the missionaries—lay beneath us.

I gasped in surprise. The 40-by-15-mile valley, studded with neat villages, resembled New England more than the last stand of Stone Age man. Everywhere I saw thatched houses, whose gardens were surrounded by stone walls. Rimming the valley were plunging gorges, giant waterfalls, terraced fields.

When we let down on a small airstrip, we were immediately engulfed by hordes of natives. Their dress consisted principally of fancy headgear of fur and feathers, necklaces of shells, boars' tusks in their noses. Their bodies were smeared with pig grease, their cheekbones daubed with colored clay.

From their midst emerged a rangy American. Erect and dignified, he looked as though he should be behind a business desk, or perhaps lecturing a college class, instead of leading one of the most perilous missionary expeditions of modern times.

This was Einar Mickelson from California.

It was on April 20, 1954, that Einar Mickelson set out by plane for Shangri-la. As he was about to take off, a Dutch official said to him: "I wouldn't go into that valley with any-

thing less than a regiment of soldiers. Hanged if I can understand what drives you missionaries!"

Mickelson just grinned. "No need to be hanged," he replied. "You could find the answer in Christ's commission to
those who try to follow Him: 'Go ye into all the world.' Or
even in Kipling. He once spoke, you remember, of 'something lost behind the ranges, lost and waiting for you—
Go!' "

The "something lost" was some 60,000 Danis, a race of
Stone Age people whose very existence was completely unknown until recent years. Among the world's last undiscov-
ered tribes, they had dwelt for untold centuries in their shut-
in Shangri-la, undisturbed by the march of time, as unaware of the existence of a "civilized world" as that world
was unaware of them.

First word of their lush and beautiful Baliem River valley
had been brought out in 1938 by Richard Archbold, an
American explorer. Confirmation of Archbold's discovery
came from three survivors of a U. S. Army plane crash in
1945, when for 50 days newspapers headlined their dramatic
rescue by glider from the floor of the valley. Then it slipped
off the front pages and became again "the valley that time
forgot."

But it was not forgotten by Einar Mickelson. Any news of
any people anywhere unreached by the Christian Gospel
was, for him, a mandate spelling "Go!" Since 1938 he had
made himself an expert on New Guinea's remoter regions,
founding for the Christian and Missionary Alliance extensive
mission operations in the Wissel Lakes area, among the
Kapauku and Moni tribes. Now he began bombarding his
movement's New York headquarters. Few salvos were

needed: the Alliance specializes in pioneering where no missionary has ever been.

Obtaining an entry permit from the Dutch colonial government was not so easy. On its maps the whole Dani area was ominously marked "uncontrolled." In its scant files the Danis were described as crafty and treacherous, cruel and vindictive. But Mickelson was undeterred. "The Gospel makes even the savage friendly," he said, pointing to the boons his missions had brought to the tribes around Wissel Lakes. When, in the summer of 1952, permission was finally granted, the Dutch government said, "Understand, you're on your own!"

Mickelson had already made two attempts to reach Shangri-la overland, and each time had been stopped by hostile tribesmen. Realizing the futility of this approach, he asked the C&MA for an amphibian plane, an expensive request. The problem was finally solved by taking it to the Alliance membership, and the funds, mostly in small gifts, were quickly subscribed.

As his missionary companion on the first flight in, Mickelson chose Lloyd Van Stone, a strapping young Texan who had fought through New Guinea with the 1st Cavalry Division. "I don't know how we'll be received," Mickelson said to Van Stone, "but there's no turning back now!" Van Stone grinned, quoted a GI axiom: "We have to go in. We don't have to come back."

At the amphibian's controls was Al Lewis of Hamilton, Ontario, a former Canadian Air Force ace. Also aboard were three Kapaukus, converts of the Wissel Lakes mission: a pastor named Elisa, his wife Ruth and their two-year-old baby. Mickelson's reasoning: since the Kapaukus were a family, their presence would assure the Danis that the invasion was a peaceful one.

Lewis let the plane down on the Baliem River. In 20 minutes the five passengers and supplies—food for 30 days, tents, lamps, radio—were unloaded, and the plane headed back.

Mickelson and Van Stone set up the radio and called their base at Sentani Lake, 150 miles away but centuries removed in time. "We're here!" they exulted. "Thank God!"

But where were the Danis? For a whole day none appeared. Did the weird silence indicate fear, or hostility?

The next day, while still getting their camp into shape, the missionaries heard a cry from Elisa, the Kapauku. They looked toward the distant hilltops to see, limned against the sky, a long line of stalwart black men, their spears held upright like so many pales of a picket fence.

But not until the following day did the Danis approach the camp. Then, abruptly materializing out of nowhere, a large group was before them—15-foot spears extended, stoneheaded battleaxes on their shoulders, bows and arrows in hand. Suddenly their leader gave a hoarse order, weapons were lowered, and the whole group surged forward with smiles and cries of *"Nahp! Nahp!"*—the Dani welcome. The missionaries repeated the cry with genuine relief, joyously credited the friendly reception to the "volumes of prayerful intercession for us by faithful groups back home."

The Danis were insatiably curious. To them, the color of the missionaries' skin was an enduring novelty. They crowded close, pinching the white faces and arms, rubbing them almost raw to see whether the "paint" would come off. The white man's gadgets, too, were an endless fascination to people who had never seen metal of any kind, nor a wheel, nor glass. Given small mirrors, they gazed entranced at their reflection, marveling that their "spirits" (which they believe to exist in the ether outside their bodies) could be captured visibly.

When the missionaries put aluminum sides on their shelter, the Danis spent hours dragging their spear ends across its corrugated surface, creating a cacophony of sound. Glass windows were equally fascinating; from morn till night the tribesmen stood like dark, living statues, staring in. When a small generator was rigged up and the first bulb lighted, they shouted, "They've got the moon in their house!"

In turn, the missionaries marveled at the Danis' intelligence and ingenuity. With only stone tools and sharpened sticks they had managed to create well-irrigated gardens, lushly full of yams, taro, spinach, beans, cucumbers, bananas. From vines, bamboo and lumber split by stone axes they had built ingenious suspension bridges, sturdy thatched houses. They had worked out a currency system using the little cowrie shell, brought in from the coast in some long-forgotten era. One shell purchases a man's labor for a half day; two shells, a bunch of bananas; three, a pig.

Family life followed ancient patterns. A man could have as many wives as he could peaceably assemble and support —or induce to support him. Wife-stealing was common; amorous men hid in the brush surrounding gardens, seized their prey as the women came to work. If caught, the attacker paid the offended husband a pig, or negotiated a wife swap. Adultery, however, was solely a male right. A man, married or single, was unrestricted in his relations with single women. But a woman was subject to severe punishment from her husband for any similar conduct. Dani women resort to the most violent extremes to induce abortion.

The missionaries found many grisly customs. One was to cut off a finger as an expression of mourning for a close relative, and cast it onto the funeral pyre. When fingers were gone, after multiple sorrows, the tips of ears were sacrificed. Few women in Shangri-la were without mutilated hands or ears.

Cannibalism was not uncommon, nor burial alive of the aged. One day the missionaries, having missed an ancient Dani, father of the mission's cook, were horrified to learn that he had been put in a hole, covered up to his neck and left to die.

Feasts, with nightlong ceremonial dancing, celebrated every special occasion, helped to drain off Dani exuberance. Missionaries had to learn which feasts to attend and which to avoid. On one occasion, while learning, they were nearly compromised. Shortly after the first mission house had been erected, a group of Danis insisted upon marking the event with a "tem" dance, described as a mild sort of flirtation waltz between unmarried young people. The missionaries were about to agree when, almost accidentally, they discovered that the dance always wound up in a free-for-all sex orgy!

And religion? The Danis had no gods, no forms of worship. They feared only "evil spirits" inhabiting the air, trees, rocks. Nothing supernatural was good, only evil. And evil spirits often vented their spleen against the living with visitations of sickness.

Of all the missionaries' devices for creating confidence and friends in Shangri-la, none was so immediately successful as medicine. Mickelson had been in the valley only a short while before word of the white man's healing magic spread from tribe to tribe. Trained in first aid, he and his colleagues spent much time treating wounds and sores, patching up broken bones and halting infection with needle-injected penicillin. Once introduced to the "shiny thorn" (the hypodermic needle), the Danis clamored for it, often inventing ailments.

The missionaries firmly believe that treating the sick, apart from its humanitarian good, "will help us to introduce Him who heals broken hearts." During my visit I watched as Tom Bozeman of Daytona Beach, Florida—recently come to the valley—treated a group of Danis for yaws, great open ulcers that eat away flesh like leprosy. After each insertion of the needle he put his hand on the patient's head and said something in the Dani language. I asked what he said. "Just a simple little prayer," he replied. "Something like: 'Lord, this man has a sore body. You are the Master of health. And You love this man. Touch him and make him well.'" Do they understand? "Perhaps not now, but some day they may remember—and thank the white man's God, not us," he replied with moving sincerity.

Shortly after coming to Shangri-la, the missionaries' medical knowledge paid off in an important way. A young brother of the most powerful chief in the area, Ukumhearik, fell out of a tree, broke his leg and suffered a concussion. For days the boy was near death, while the witch-doctor vainly performed his rites.

Ukumhearik, a regal potentate with 20 wives and 10,000 followers, sent for Van Stone. "He is going to die, white Tuan," said the chief. "You help save?" Van Stone sent the witch-doctor away, set the broken leg, hovered over the lad for days, then persuaded the chief to let him take the boy by plane to the hospital at Hollandia. Within two weeks the missionary was back, bearing a completely healed youngster. Ukumhearik never forgot the good deed. His memory of it was, quite literally, a lifesaver to the missionaries on a number of tense occasions.

The witch-doctor, who had been a troublemaker for the mission, deemed it wise henceforth to be helpful too. One day when Van Stone was stricken with malaria, he came to the mission house. "Me help sick Tuan," he said, beginning his incantations. Van Stone interrupted the mumbo-jumbo to say, "I'll be all right. Jesus will heal me." The witch-doctor went on waving his leaves and twiddling his fingers above the missionary. "Me help Jesus!" he grunted.

When someone from the outside observed that "the whole Baliem venture is suspended by two pretty slender threads —Dani friendship and one lone plane," one of the missionaries replied quietly, "Our dependence and confidence have always been in Him who 'hangeth the world on nothing.'"

The slenderness of that second thread was demonstrated when, for a period of five months, the plane could not land because of low water in the Baliem and could fly in only once every three weeks to drop supplies by parachute. It was even more tragically proved one day when, in attempting a supply flight during bad weather, Pilot Al Lewis missed the pass and crashed into a cloud-hooded peak. The loss of pilot and plane was a blow; for weeks the mission was isolated until another plane, land based, could be obtained and an airstrip built.

Dani friendliness too, it early became plain, was a brittle

and often twisted thread. Their moods could change in a flash from easy amiability to truculence to blood thirst. Such perverse switches were usually sparked by either their inbred love for inter-tribal fighting or some inadvertent violation of their ancient taboos and superstitions.

The missionaries had not been long at their first rough camp when they discovered that they had settled in a sort of no man's land between two warring tribes: the people of the valley and the hill-dwellers. One night in July 1954 the hill people raided the river gardens to steal sugar cane. The next day, while a few visitors from the hills were curiously poking about the mission camp, they were suddenly ambushed by river warriors. Arrows and spears flew about the camp; two hill-dwellers were killed, another fell while fleeing. Stunned at first by this violence, Van Stone grabbed his shotgun, fired into the air, frightened the attackers away, then rushed up the hill down which 300 hill warriors were charging.

When the leader advanced on him, spear poised, the missionary said quietly, "You have your spear, I have mine. Here's what mine can do!"—and fired a blast that tore away the branches of a tree. The warriors retired in sulky haste. That night the missionaries went up the hill to treat the wounded and bring consolation to the bereaved.

During the next few weeks tempestuous battles blazed again and again—with more dead and wounded left on the missionaries' doorstep. By November Mickelson and his group decided it was the better part of valor—as well as Christian strategy—to move. So, on Thanksgiving, they abandoned the camp and established a new station four miles south, at Hitigima, close to a large concentration of Danis.

The author making friends with Chief Ukumhearik (*left*), undisputed ruler of 10,000 Danis and husband to 20 wives, and his witch-doctor at Hitigima in New Guinea. (Chapter I)

The picture which, when shown to the Stone-Age Danis, brought to the "Shangri-La" missionaries their closest brush with death. (see page 36)

Dani tribesmen preparing fire for feast celebrating victory in one of the tribal wars that rage constantly in the Baliem Valley. (Chapter I)

Missionary Tom Bozeman inoculating with penicillin a victim of yaws, most prevalent disease in "Shangri-La"

One of the missionaries sighed in a letter home: "It's going to take a while to teach the Dani to love his enemies, not to steal his wife or pig, not to whack him with an ax or pierce him with a spear."

At the mission one day some Danis were curiously looking through an American magazine. When one seemed to be dwelling overlong at an illustration, a missionary leaned over, snatched the magazine away. He tore out the page and crumpled it: it was a picture of Hercules decapitating the Hydra. "These people," he muttered, "don't need any suggestions on how to make mayhem more efficient!"

Most Dani customs either lead to war or flow from it. Rigid boundary lines separate the hundreds of valley tribes; to cross them means death. But to the Dani, risking death is better than boredom. And Danis, the missionaries soon learned, bore easily.

Cannibalism is practiced only on strong and valiant enemies—to gain their virtues. On one occasion, hearing that a young warrior had been badly wounded and was in the hands of the enemy in a nearby village, Van Stone hurried over to offer medical treatment. At the village edge, he saw a column of smoke rising. He was told, "You no need go; him now being roasted. Big feast tonight!"

Here, more than once, the missionaries learned how suddenly Dani amiability could change to bloodthirst. Their closest brush with disaster came a year ago when three Dani girls who had been helping to make an airstrip were drowned while crossing the Baliem River. Going to console the mothers, Van Stone found the families had been worked into a fever of excitement by a few troublemakers.

At the funeral next day the people sat swaying and moaning, their black faces contorted, their hands quivering on their spears. Hostility rose to passionate pitch when one of the mothers dramatically whacked off two of her fingers with a stoneheaded ax and flung them into Van Stone's face.

The missionary pushed his way through the screaming mob, sought out Ukumhearik.

"My people say you have brought only trouble," said the chief. "They demand your death. But I try to help you."

He addressed the people: "This is my friend. Before missionaries came, you were poor—no shells, no axes, no cloth. Now we have all these."

The people shouted back angrily, wanting no part of the olive branch. Ukumhearik lifted his hand. "Listen," he said. "Big bird come to save white man." Sure enough, it was the mission plane coming in on an emergency run. Frightened, the Danis fell on the ground, and the chief whisked the missionary out of danger. By the next day hostility had died as quickly as it had flared.

One evening, three months after the three girls' death, danger flared again. The missionaries were projecting colored slides on the wall of their house. As the Danis recognized themselves, they laughed and shouted, "My spirit!" Then inadvertently a slide was inserted of a group containing two of the dead girls. Immediately the Danis prostrated themselves on the ground. When one cried out, "They've got dead spirits in that box!" a fearful murmur crackled through the crowd like dry grass aflame. Sensing a riot in the making, the missionaries stopped the show, sent for the tribe's leaders, spent hours patiently demonstrating how pictures were made and reproduced. The incident passed. But henceforth the

missionaries carefully screened their pictures prior to projecting them.

Despite such alarums, the missionaries managed gradually
to build up confidence in their intentions, nibbling away at
native hostility with a multitude of good deeds.

Most formidable obstacle was the Dani tongue, unlike any
encountered elsewhere. To help hurdle it, a talented missionary linguist, Myron Bromley of Meadville, Pennsylvania,
was brought in. Equipped with a notebook and dogged de-
termination, Bromley wandered among the people, listening
to the Dani speech, his pencil busy. With a tape recorder, he
sat for hours pointing to objects, having people repeat the
words for them over and over. At first the Danis were puzzled that anyone could not comprehend their tongue, would
put their faces up close to Bromley's, speaking loud and
clear as to a retarded child.

From such patient attempts to "unscramble Babel" he
acquired a large Dani vocabulary in an incredibly short time,
then produced a series of lessons for the other missionaries.
Within a few weeks all were fluent enough to converse.
Mastery of grammar and syntax took longer. Eventually,
however, the hitherto unrecorded tongue was reduced to
primer materials, and a pilot teaching project was started
with a small group of Danis.

The problem of getting the Christian message across was
at first discouraging. For one thing, the Dani language con-
tains no words or idioms for such essential terms as "love,"
"sin," "grace," "salvation." After his initial attempts to explain
God's love for sinning humanity, Bromley reported, "The
people looked at me with as much comprehension as if I
were talking in Latin about the price of corn in Iowa." He

concluded, "Perhaps the Lord wants to remind us that this message is not something to be casually huckstered."

Meanwhile, the men went on treks through the valley to make friends with other tribes. At first this provoked angry protests from the Hitigimans. They rolled their eyes to express terror, bit their arms and pointed to their stomachs to indicate "cannibals." Some even tried physically to restrain them. But the missionaries pushed on across the boundaries, concluding that "the uniform reluctance to let us leave is probably influenced more by their desire to retain the benefits of our presence than to protect us." The Danis in other areas, they found, were mostly friendly. In one spot, however, Bromley and Elisa were thrown to the ground and spears were placed against their throats. Sure that his end was near, Elisa rolled his eyes heavenward and prayed, "Well, Jesus, here I come!" Bromley, thinking fast, redeemed their lives with a few cowrie shells.

On another occasion, Van Stone and two others had an even closer call. They had taken a small boat up the Baliem to survey some of the other tribes when, ashore for a while, they were suddenly attacked with flying arrows and spears. Declarations of peaceful aims availing nothing, they retreated to the boat and paddled rapidly away. Feeling what he thought was a branch caught against his knee, Van Stone broke it off—only to find an arrow had pierced his leg. It had to be pulled out with pliers, and he was laid up for days.

This incident, following on the heels of other frightening scrapes, accomplished what months of wartime fighting in the South Pacific could not do: it put Van Stone on the brink of a crack-up. Startled at the depth of his fears, he knew he had to lick them or be through as a missionary. As soon as he could walk, he forced himself to go back into the same territory where he had been shot.

"As I approached the spot," he says, "I felt a terror creeping over me that was almost diabolical." He prayed for strength, repeated, "Lo, I am with you always," and, "Be strong and of good courage." His fears fell away. The formerly sinister tribe met him peaceably, promised to receive any missionaries who would come later. "From that day I have felt no twinge of fear," he testifies, "even in the tensest situations."

After harrowing months, more missionaries were brought in. Also, wives joined husbands, and in many cases families came too. The coming of white women was of strategic importance. Dani women, who had stayed shyly in the background until then, flocked around the mission, giving the wives a chance to go to work on their superstitions, teach them child care, sanitation, household arts.

First white woman in Hitigima was Darlene Rose, wife of Gerry Rose of Bristol, Tennessee, who joined the group in December 1954. She caused a bug-eyed sensation. Hundreds of Baliem belles ran mutilated fingers through her fair hair, pinched and rubbed her skin. Bewildered, she asked her husband, "Am I being examined or tenderized?"

Chief Ukumhearik threw a big feast in her honor, seated her beside him before mountains of roast pig and yams. Served a choice rib, she was wondering where to begin when Ukumhearik helpfully took it from her. With great decorum he dug meat from bone with his long and dirty fingernails, rolled the morsel on his pig-greased thigh, then flicked it into her mouth. She gagged but managed to swallow, graciously smiling her appreciation; later commented, "And I never even had a stomach-ache!" Made the chief's "daughter" that night, she thereafter was dubbed the "white princess" by the Danis.

With the coming of the wives and children, Dani periods of capricious rancor became less frequent. More time could be devoted to solidifying friendly relations with other clans, preparing to set up schools and clinics. Yet even today every missionary knows that the natives' friendliness cannot be taken for granted, so ingrained is their superstition and so mercurial their temperament.

A tragic reminder of this fact occurred in November 1956, at Wissel Lakes. A band of unconverted Kapaukus, blaming the missions for an epidemic of disease among pigs, descended on the settlements, killing an Indonesian pastor and his wife, also two children of another worker. They burned to the ground a school and several mission buildings, then hacked the mission airplane to pieces.

Mickelson's aim from the beginning was not only the creation of a well-based Christian society in Shangri-La but a strong indigenous leadership when white leaders will no longer be needed. Mistakes of early missions were carefully avoided: Mickelson told me he had no intention of stifling native initiative and ingenuity, of replacing Dani culture with Western ways, or of clothing nakedness with Mother Hubbards.

The delay in making converts bothered Mickelson not a bit. To begin with, it was enough to impress upon the Danis that the white man was their friend, to bring them physical healing, to teach them peaceful ways and the arts of better living. "Our job is to live with the Danis, share their life, earn their love," he said to me. "If Christianity cannot make its impression through love and kindness and helpfulness, then it's not what we know it to be."

After two years in the valley, the Alliance had ten missionaries and their families at three thriving stations in the valley —each with its own airstrip hacked out by hundreds of friendly Danis. And early in 1957, the Dutch territorial government, satisfied that Shangri-la had finally been "pacified" sufficiently for the establishment of a government post in the valley, began construction of a 1500-meter airstrip capable of handling large planes. Moreover, the government promised to help subsidize schools and hospitals.

About the missionaries and their work, Dutch officials are now lyrical. Says Dr. Victor de Bruijn, director of the Bureau for Native Affairs for Netherlands New Guinea: "Before the boons of civilization can be brought to Stone Age natives, a revolution in their mental attitudes has to be effected. That's what Christian missions are dramatically accomplishing in Shangri-la. These missionaries know far more about this part of New Guinea and its people than does the government. We are glad to follow their lead."

Would the government have trouble recruiting personnel to man its post? De Bruijn thought so. "To impel a man to live and work in so primitive a region," he says, "he must have a song to sing. Missionaries have the song—their courageous faith—and the noblest of human motives: to do good for the people."

To that tune, Christian missions for centuries have marched against darkness and superstition the world around. Today, in Shangri-la, that song is ringing clear throughout the "valley that time forgot."

II

He Gave Sight to 100,000

The surgeon in charge of a mission hospital on India's wild North-West Frontier was jarred awake, the night of May 30, 1935, by a thundering roar. The room rocked and pitched, to the sound of fearful crashing and the screams of patients in his nearby hospital. Before he could struggle from his cot amid falling debris, a huge weight knocked him unconscious.

This was the Quetta earthquake, one of the most disastrous in world history. In a few seconds it reduced the city of 60,000 to rubble, killing outright some 24,000 of its people.

The 60-year-old missionary came to consciousness amid the deathly silence following the quake. Then, suddenly, he heard a shout through the darkness. It was his son, also a doctor and his assistant, who too had miraculously escaped death. The surgeon painfully lifted his head and called out in his high-pitched voice, "For Pete's sake, Harry, get me out of here. There's work to be done!"

Frantically the son tore at the hill of rubble, and in 15 minutes the two were organizing rescue efforts. The hospital compound with its facilities for 130 patients, two operating theaters, laboratory, large dispensary and X-ray plant —built up from almost nothing through 35 agonizing years of

42

effort—was a shambles. Many of the patients and hospital staff members were dead or dying. The missionary surgeon limped about, furiously bandaging the wounded, directing the removal of hundreds of corpses, giving thousands of injections to stave off an epidemic of cholera.

Meeting perils was nothing new to Dr. Henry Tristram Holland. When I saw him, in 1957, at 82 years of age he was still meeting them—and bringing Christian profit from them. A man small of stature and puckish of countenance, his unspectacular appearance belies his spectacular record and repute as one of the world's foremost eye surgeons. During his 56 years in the border country between Afghanistan and what is now Pakistan, he gave back sight to more than 100,000 persons.

In recognition of his life-service to the tribespeople of the North-West Frontier, and for his contribution to ophthalmology, Holland was knighted in 1936 by King Edward VIII —the only surviving missionary knight since Sir Wilfred Grenfell's death.

In Sir Henry's youth there was nothing to forecast him in the role of either knight or missionary. Son of an Anglican country parson, young Henry decided to "go into medicine to get out of the church." While studying at Edinburgh University, however, he fell in with students intending to become medical missionaries. Moreover, many of the medical faculty, he found, were devoted Christians, active in the University Christian Medical Association. Here he was impressed by such speakers as Henry Drummond, propounder of love as "The Greatest Thing in the World," and Charles Studd, a famous cricket player. One day he noted over a mantel a cryptic motto, *"Not for ours only."* Asking its meaning, he found it was from I John 2:2—"And he is the propitiation for our sins: and not for ours only, but also for the sins of the whole world." Responding to the summons to selfless living, Henry finally applied to the Church Missionary Society, a foreign missions arm of the Church of England.

Holland offered to go to Nigeria, but was told, "We're sending you to Quetta." Mystified, he demanded, "Where's that?" He soon found out. The North-West Frontier, with Quetta as its southern bastion, was a rough land of Kiplingesque people and storied history. Its rocky desert wastes, barren hills and bloodstained passes—such as the famed Khyber—had for 3500 years known the tread of invading armies. In this no man's land he found a racial mosaic of nomadic Brahuis, swarthy Baluchis, marauding Pathan tribes devoted to blood feuds and banditry. The Frontier tribesman was a strange medley of the swashbuckling brigand—cruel, treacherous, fanatical—and the brave, proud, individualistic lover of freedom, deeply religious according to his lights. Tall, bearded, with deep-set fiery eyes and hawk noses, the Pathans disdained all laws laid down by modern governments, ruling themselves by tribal "Customary Laws" that were old before America was discovered.

Because their land could not produce crops, the tribesmen "farmed" the passes by raids on passing caravans. Almost every family had a blood feud going. The tribes were nomadic, grazing their camels, flocks and herds in the Baluch and Afghan uplands all summer, then streaming through the passes toward the plains of India in the winter. To keep these hordes of free-ranging peoples in check, strong British garrisons policed the Frontier.

The mission at Quetta, started in 1886, was one of a chain

of stations begun not by missionaries but by British officers
and enlisted men with an enlightened idea of Christianity's
responsibility in colonial rule. They raised funds among
themselves, petitioned the Church of England to send out
clergy and doctors, then supported them for years.

Among such Christian soldiers was Major General Sir
Herbert Edwardes, who stood one day at Khyber Pass and
warned his men not to think "this immense India has been
given to our little England for no other purpose than our
aggrandizement. Empires come into existence for purposes
of the world's Creator."

Young Henry Holland reached Quetta in May 1900, to
find a plague raging in Karachi, with people dying in the
streets. On the long 400-mile journey to Quetta, he traveled
by pony, camel and on foot across the hot sands of the Sind
Desert, trekking with the tall, hawk-nosed tribesmen carrying their homemade rifles with curving stocks inlaid with
brass and their great curved swords bright with semi-pre-
cious stones.

The mission station seemed to him an audacity, a tiny but
brave assertion that Christianity cares—for both body and
soul. Such caring, he soon learned, could be costly.

Aroused by mullahs, the powerful Moslem religious leaders, tribesmen often went on rampages, murdering Afghan
converts to Christianity, Indians and British as apostates in
Islam's eyes. To the fanatics, the killing of an "infidel" was a
pious act. Prior to Holland's coming and during his first years
on the Frontier, scores of missionaries and their converts
provided Moslem warriors with such passports to paradise.

Converts to Christianity suffered even more wholesale re-
prisals. On the Frontier it was a proud Moslem boast that

"no Afghan turned Christian has ever returned to his own country and lived." One convert, son of a Moslem judge in Quetta, was seized, spirited in chains to Kabul, the Afghanistan capital, cruelly beaten then given a chance to recant. When he refused, one of his arms was hacked off, then the other. Still refusing to recant, he was beheaded. However, a witness to the man's martyrdom later wrote Holland: "The remembrance of the light and peace in Abdul Karin's face has haunted me through the years. Tell me the secret of it." This man too was converted—and later executed for his new-found faith.

Holland prayed nightly that "I may scorn the way of safety, so that Thy will may be done." To his hospital staff he said: "If we Christians cannot out-live and out-love any other religion, we don't deserve to win."

He left no patient in doubt as to the motivation behind his treatment. Before each operation he would say a short prayer, endeavor to make every healing technique a "testimony to the tender mercy of God." Asked why he mixed Christian evangelization with medical treatment, he snapped: "I am a *missionary* doctor. The Christian medical man who says everything about the body and nothing about the soul is not doing his full duty."

When a prominent Moslem leader hotly demanded why the mission tried to convert his people, Holland deftly took the wind out of his angry sails by saying, "We love your people, and so we want them to have the best—in religion as in medicine. Since we think Christianity the best of religions, we cannot be selfish with it any more than we can withhold from those we love the best medical skills and medicines we have."

When the 25-year-old doctor first came to Quetta his hospital boasted only a few beds and almost no modern equipment. His own experience in surgery, as a student at Edinburgh, had been limited to opening a few abscesses and presiding at a birth or two. But such was the pitiful plight of the people, particularly during plagues and epidemics, that he soon was treating almost all ailments in the medical glossary. He wrote home: "If you ever see P.C. after my name, it won't mean I've been made Privy Councilor; it'll stand for piles and cataracts!"

Cataracts particularly. This ailment was common along the Frontier, and the pathos of the blind touched him deeply. He soon discovered not only a special facility but his greatest satisfaction in curing blindness. And as word of his skill got about, tribespeople came in droves to be cured.

One day an old couple, both completely blinded by double cataracts, stumbled into his compound. They had not seen each other for years. Holland operated, then placed them in beds side by side in the hospital ward. Days later, when the bandages were removed simultaneously, they looked at each other with first unbelief, then sheer enchantment. As the two old people went into each other's arms, tears of joy flowing down their faces, Holland wept with them.

Whole families would arrive at the compound, bringing along children, animals, chickens. A patient quartered in one of the wards would tether his camel outside, and one or more relatives would bed down beside him. Some tribesmen, who had never slept under anything but a tent roof, balked at the wards. For the sake of tradition and family solidarity, Dr. Holland always accommodated them. One family, with a small son needing a bladder stone removal, slept in their bullock cart—with the bull—in the compound outside. In a temporary shelter serving as a pile ward, the doctor one day found a horse tethered next to a patient. Humorously, he asked if the horse suffered from the same complaint—and let him stay.

The Quetta hospital, growing without plan or design, became a helter-skelter assortment of annexes and scattered family wards. After the earthquake, the present modern, reinforced-brick 200-bed hospital, with four operating theaters, delivery room, X-ray laboratory and nurses' training school was erected—mostly from funds raised personally by Sir Henry during a tour of England and a public appeal put on in his behalf by the London *Times*.

A further impressive monument to Sir Henry's skill with both lancet and religious diplomacy is the famous Shikarpur Hospital 200 miles southeast of Quetta. One of the largest eyes clinics in the world, it can care for as many as 600 patients at a time.

Shikarpur, an exclusive Hindu city, had been closed tight to Christian missionaries. But in October 1909, Holland was approached by Seth Hiranand, a Shikarpur banker and philanthropist who for some time had been sending patients to Quetta. "Why do you not come to my city?" he asked. "I will provide many patients, pay all expenses."

Arriving in the forbidden city, Holland found hundreds of blind and sick swarming about the grounds of Hiranand's estate. He set up an operating theater on the large scimitar-shaped verandah and went to work, fighting flies and dust and clamorous patients. He stayed three weeks, performed more than 400 operations. Before he left, the banker brought him a large bag of rupees and a proposition. "Doctor Sahib,"

he said, "as you have seen, there are many here who need
your skills. You will come again next year—perhaps annually?"

Cannily, the little surgeon replied: "I will, on condition
that you build a suitable hospital, housing for patients, and
underwrite all expenses." The banker agreed readily. Squat-
ting on the floor, Holland drew preliminary plans in the
verandah's dust. That done, he arose. "There's one other condition," he said. "If I come, I must have the right to preach
Christianity here."

When the conditions of the project became known, a city-
wide uproar arose. A big mass-meeting denounced the plan
for Christian infiltration. Hiranand sat through the angry
speeches, then rose to win the day by quietly saying, "If
you will find a surgeon as great as the Doctor Sahib, one
who will heal our blind and sick, and yet not preach Christianity, I will agree with you. Shall the thousands of our
people who need treatment be denied it by our prejudices?"

Getting news of the victory, Holland chuckled: "I'll bet
Shikarpur is the first city in the world to be opened to Christianity at the point of a cataract knife."

Next year, he found in that city a beautiful little hospital
ready for him, with two well-equipped operating rooms,
plentiful housing accommodations—and 500 new patients
waiting. The reputation of the Shikarpur clinic, in full-tilt
operation each January-February, spread rapidly, until Holland and his associates were performing as many as 1200
cataract operations and 2000 other major surgical procedures
during the six weeks the clinic operated. Leading ophthal-
mologists traveled across the world to observe the Holland
techniques.

Among them were many Americans. One, Dr. Derrick Vail of Northwestern University Medical School, tells of finding Sir Henry's aura everywhere about the hospital and its compound. "I was not fully prepared to grasp at once the striking character of this dynamic and expert eye surgeon. But in a few moments his simple and compassionate nature, radiating from his inner warmth, embraced me and I knew that here was a very great and good man."

Another American took Holland back to the States with him for a vacation in 1928, pressed him to join his staff to ultimately succeed him as head of one of the Midwest's largest eye-ear-nose-and-throat hospitals. When Holland shook his head, the eminent doctor offered a fabulous salary, saying archly, "I'm told that every man has his price, Sir Henry." The missionary surgeon laughed. "I'm afraid you've been misinformed. You can't put a price tag on a fellow's love for his people."

During his long career, he was offered many other high medical posts. Always he turned them down.

Holland early found that his compulsion to bring sight and healing to the needy could not be contained by Quetta and the several out-stations he established. Nor could his adventurous spirit. With British political and military officers he argued that if he could go with them, "throwing pills about and applying the proper sort of ointments," he might "help to reduce the temperatures" of troublesome tribesmen.

He proved his point one day at a remote village on the Baluch-Persian frontier where a team of British agents had to deal with a difficult border bandit named Dost Mahomed. The bandit, whose murdering and pillaging had thrown the whole area into chaos, rode up on a prancing stallion and

with five of his sub-chiefs marched into the desert tent for
the meeting, rifles in hand, bandoliers of cartridges criss-
crossing their sunburned chests, surly and defiant.

While the negotiations went on, getting nowhere, Holland
slipped out, slung a medicine chest over his shoulders and
crossed the frontier into the walled city where 1500 of Mahomed's followers were encamped. For hours he treated the
sick, and when he returned to the place of conference 300
of them came with him, singing praises for the help he'd
brought. The bandit came out, still fuming at the Britishers'
demands. But when he saw the crowd of his own people,
happy over Holland's ministrations, he and his men laid down
their guns. The British agents used the truce to depart hur-
riedly. Afterward, Holland was told, "Dost Mahomed came
to the conference determined to kill the whole party. You
stopped him cold."

Alone, or with a mission colleague, he went out among
the tribespeople in areas where seldom a white man had ever
been seen. Through the craggy hills and sunblistered valleys,
he would travel for days on pony back, or on a riding camel
—"the most uncomfortable conveyance known to man." When
he came upon a cluster of glowering Pathans, he would dis-
mount to treat diseases, patch up wounds, perform delicate
eye operations.

For these proud people, whom powerful British forces
could not conquer, he conceived a lasting affection. And
they for him. He moved through their forbidden areas unarmed—and unharmed. While he performed his operations,
the tribesmen would gather around curiously. He employed
them as screens from the dust and sand, put fans in their
hands to keep the flies away.

To win the tribesmen's confidence, he joined them in riding, fishing, shooting. In appreciation for his services, they
would come at day's end to his campfire, offering with great
dignity gifts of their poor best: a joint of mutton, fruit, a
hand-made rug, a trinket.

On one tour, he had just finished treating a tribe and was
about to go when news came that a band of bloodthirsty
Afghan outlaws had slipped over the border and were in the
vicinity. But, he was assured, "They will not harm you."
Later he learned that his friends had sent outriders ahead to
throw around him an invisible circle of protection.

Wherever he went the tribesmen would seek him out.
On one occasion, while on a brief holiday in the Himalayan
foothills, a group of Pathans came leading a woman with
double cataracts. They pointed to her, saying simply, "Doctor
Sahib . . ." The only instruments he had with him were a
pair of iris forceps and a cataract knife. But from the wife of
a companion he borrowed nail scissors, tweezers and a cro-
chet hook; from a hairpin he improvised an instrument to
hold the eye open. Then, sterilizing his strange instruments,
he went to work. Five days later, when the bandages were
removed, the operation proved a complete success.

During another trip deep into the desert he came to a
small oasis, found a cluster of Baluchis hovered over a man
groaning in pain and near death. The man had fallen 30 feet
from the top of a date palm tree, badly ruptured his urethra;
his bladder was distended almost to the bursting point.
Having only primitive surgical instruments with him, Holland punctured the bladder, contrived a drainage tube from
the metal case of a clinical thermometer, smoothed it down
with files and emery board, and bandaged him up. Being

60 miles from the nearest railhead, 140 miles from the nearest hospital, the little doctor hoisted his patient onto a camel for the long desert trek, breathing a prayer that sepsis would not set in. Arriving at the railroad station after 24 hours with his patient, he found that the next train was not due for 36 hours. Keeping his patient alive by sheer will power, they reached the hospital two long hot days later. Holland operated again, found the wound aseptic, his man on the road to recovery. "God is great!" chorused the Baluchis.

His reputation spread among the highly placed as well as the lowly. He treated the Rajah of Shigar at his capital 200 miles from the border of Tibet, on one occasion was flown to Kabul to save the sight of the King of Afghanistan. One day he received a message from one of the most powerful of the Frontier chieftains, the fabulous Wali of Swat, noted for his antipathy for missionaries. But his need was greater than his intolerance: he was going blind—would the Doctor Sahib come?

Holland traveled by foot through the passes beyond Malakand, where the Wali and his people had attacked the British and where Sir Winston Churchill served as a war correspondent. Finally he came to a setting like a page out of *The Arabian Nights*. After saying the first Christian prayer ever heard in the palace, Sir Henry operated successfully on the Wali's eyes. Afterward, they became fast friends, often went hunting together.

Not the least of Sir Henry Holland's achievements for Pakistan and the North-West Frontier is his role in bringing Moslem women into the 20th century. When he first came, women had their place—in the rigid seclusion of "purdah."

Wives were bought like cattle. Hospitals were "men only" institutions. Sir Henry's mission established a hospital for women in the Quetta compound, convinced husbands that it was an economic waste to allow a wife to wither and die.

One of his weirdest tasks was the replacing of women's noses. Extremely jealous, the Pathan's tradition allowed him to chop off a wife's nose at the slightest suspicion of infidelity. Later, discovering her innocence, he was likely to regret his action, bring her to the hospital for repairs. One, when told that the operation would cost 60 shillings, hesitated until the doctor asked, "Is it not worth the money to have a wife with a nose?" The tribesman replied, "That's a hard question, Doctor Sahib. You see, for 75 shillings I can buy a new wife!"

Sir Henry also gave Moslem and Hindu womanhood an important boost up the social and professional ladder by his program for training nurses and hospital technicians. In 1900, the idea of any proper Moslem girl working outside the home, let alone in a hospital, was abhorrent. Holland, always hard pressed to staff his hospital, put constant stress on the dignity of serving one's fellows in need, on a people's responsibility to help care for its own.

For years the backbone of his nursing staff came from the outcast and depressed classes, many of them second generation Christians. His mission's nursing schools were the first to give women not only training but graduate standing and certification. Today the daughters of Pakistan's best families are being trained as doctors and nurses.

For more than a half century Sir Henry worked toward the the day when his hospital could be taken over completely by indigenous leaders. "It is always a missionary's happiest achievement," he says, "when a Christian institution can be handed over to nationals, and is no longer a work done *for* them but *by* them."

In 1939 Sir Henry reached his society's retirement age, 65 —with no hankering to quit. Shortage of doctors in World War II gave him the excuse to ask for an "extension for the duration." He managed to extend the extension to eight years.

In the spring of 1948, when he was 74, having seen his son Ronald succeed him at Quetta, he took what he thought was his final departure from the land and people to whom he had given his life. But he had hardly got back to England —muttering darkly at the "foolishness of a system that retires a man in his prime"—when word came that tribal chiefs had made up a purse to bring him back for a period each year. Ever since, he has spent his winters on the Frontier, his summers going up and down England recruiting missionaries and stimulating British youth to selfless service.

Speaking to an assembly of London young people in 1956, he chided them for modern youth's preoccupation with security, their hesitancy toward pioneering. "The grave is secure," he said, "but terribly dull. Serve your age well and security will take care of itself!"

When someone once asked why, with talents that would have brought him vast material gains, he gave himself so selflessly to healing the hurt of mankind, he replied, "Remember what a chap named Mallory said when he was asked why he wanted to climb Mt. Everest? *'Because it's there!'* That's my answer, too."

III

Skipper of the *Morning Star*

When the storm struck—one of those violent eruptions of wind and wave for which the mid-Pacific is noted—the 60-foot ketch was tossed around like an eggshell nearing Niagara Falls. Drenched with spray, I clung to the gunwale —and forgot my fears, watching the 65-year-old woman at her post behind the helmsman. Clad in oilskins, her white hair whipping from beneath her sou'wester, she was issuing calm commands which sent her dark-hued crewmen scuttling about the plunging decks and up the crazily weaving rigging. She might have been giving directions to a maid at tea-time.

This was the *Morning Star VII*, latest in a long line of fabled missionary ships which have plied the waters of Micronesia for the past century, serving the churches and people of its myriad islands and atolls—and helping make the Marshalls and Carolines among the most thoroughly Christianized areas in the world.

And this was the equally fabled Eleanor Wilson, lady skipper and ordained minister, whose name is known from Guam in the Marianas to Kapingamarangi in the Carolines, from Eniwetok to Ebon in the Marshalls, and whose ship's wake today is inscribing one of the most audacious pages in missionary history. To me the gentle Miss Wilson seemed better

suited to doing petit point in some Boston Back Bay drawing room than to piloting a storm-battered ship, with only a
native crew for company, through some of the most dangerous waters in the world.

That night, the tempest over and the *Morning Star* back
on course, we sat on the hatchcover beneath a sky whose stars
seemed close enough for plucking while Eleanor Wilson
traced for me the unpredictable paths that had brought her
to this unusual career. Born into a New England family
heavy with the names of educators and college presidents,
she went to Simmons College, became secretary to a pro-
fessor at Massachusetts Institute of Technology. Nothing
was further from her mind than being a missionary, unless
it was being a ship captain. As a young woman she took to
religion lightly, and to the sea with distaste.

But when, in 1921, a friend challenged her by saying,
"Eleanor, you're now 30, and what are you doing to make
the world better?" she began some serious thinking. She enrolled in New York's Biblical Seminary, became a YWCA
director of education.

Two years later she took her longest step away from
Beacon Hill. Offered the presidency of Women's Evangelistic
School in Kobe, Japan, she accepted—with a reservation.
She prayed, "Lord, if I get seasick on the way out, I'll know
I've made a mistake." Since her only previous experience on
the sea had been agonizing, she was certain that this test of
her "calling" guaranteed an early return home. But amaz-
ingly, her stomach stubbornly refused her the alibi; she felt
not a moment of nausea—then or ever again.

In 1933 she was summoned back to Boston as associate
secretary for the American Board of Commissioners for For-

eign Missions. Her job: to find missionaries for far and difficult places. To her desk one day came an appeal for a teacher willing to go out to Kusaie in the Caroline Islands, then under Japanese mandate. "When I found recruiting difficult," she says, "my New England conscience demanded to know why I was asking others to go where I was unwilling to go myself." She went, paying her own fare and taking all her savings to sustain her for a year. Except for the war years she has been in the islands ever since, teaching in mission schools on Kusaie, Truk and Ponape in the eastern Carolines, at Jaluit, Uliga and Rong Rong in the Marshalls.

She became a lady skipper, abruptly, in 1950. A sailor from the U. S. Coast Guard station at Rong Rong came running through the palms, a cablegram in his hand, and saluted with exaggerated smartness. "Gotta call you Captain now, ma'am," he grinned. "You just got yourself a ship!"

The cablegram said that the missionary who had been skippering the *Morning Star VI* had been called home. The ship was berthed at Kwajalein; there was nobody else available to serve as captain. The message said, in effect, "You're it!" She read the cablegram three times before she realized that she, who knew nothing about navigation and held in respectful fear the unmarked, reef-ridden, shark-infested waters beyond the placid lagoons, was being handed the job. What in heaven's name was the board thinking of?

She had no time to ponder. "Better get ready, ma'am," said the sailor. "I'm to take you by launch to Uliga, where you can catch the Navy plane to Kwaj."

At Kwajalein her heart sank further when she saw the *Star*. Its sails were rotting, its auxiliary engine out of repair, its radio generator corroded and useless. And the crew was

plainly aghast that she was taking over. She summoned them
to the afterdeck. "The ways of the Lord," she said (adding
under her breath, "and of the board"), "are past understanding. But you all know how our churches and people have
depended upon 'God's little white ships' to bring them the
Gospel, supplies and transportation for students and pastors.
If the Lord means for us—you and me together—to sail the
Star and do His work, He will protect us. Let's remember
Psalm 97: 'The Lord reigneth . . . let the multitude of isles
be glad thereof.'"

Reassured that Deity was still in control but visibly un-
certain that with her at the helm the isles would ever be
seen by them, let alone be "made glad," the crewmen muttered, "Amen." She surveyed their craggy, dark faces a moment, then added, "I'm going to see if the United States
Navy will help us make the *Star* seaworthy. Meanwhile, I
want you to scrub the decks, polish all brass, spray the
cabins with DDT—and make God's ship one He won't be
ashamed of!"

Glad of the chance to sink their sorrows in work, the crew
soon had the little ship spick-and-span. They went further.
Suddenly conscious that the *Star* had no "head" that would
work, during her absence ashore one day they constructed
on the fantail a crude but practical structure of canvas and
two-by-fours—then modestly averted their eyes and retreated
forward whenever she headed aft.

The next six weeks were maddeningly frustrating. Even
with the willing help of Navy men, it took endless days to get
new parts for the engine, patches for the sails, repairs for
chronometer and generator. To improve the time, Eleanor
Wilson studied Mixter's *Primer of Navigation*, and talked an

Air Force navigator into teaching her how to use a sextant and plot a course. After several shakedown runs in the atoll's 60-mile lagoon to try out her new knowledge, she laid a course to Jaluit, 200 miles southeast, and headed for the open sea. Going through a pass, a sailor on another ship hailed her, "Where you bound, ma'am?" When she told him he shouted, "Who's your navigator?" She jabbed a forefinger proudly at herself. "Wow!" he exclaimed. "I'm glad I'm not aboard!"

She delivered her ship to its port without mishap.

Nevertheless, those first months intimately acquainted her with the haunting hazards of her new job. Of sailing through seas without lighthouses or buoys to mark the channels, or shore lights to guide her in. Of the treachery of green water indicating reefs that could rip the bottom from her craft. Of menacing coral heads just beneath the surface of otherwise innocent water. Of sudden squalls and tricky ocean currents that could throw her miles off course. Of blanketing clouds that hid the horizon and blocked from sight the low-lying islands, most of which were but a few feet above sea level. Of engine failure that seemed to come oftenest when approaching narrow passages through reefs into the safety of calm lagoons.

For instance, there was the time when, on the way to Ponape via Ujelang, both her engine and the winds died. Becalmed for three days, she was unaware that ocean currents were drifting them toward danger until suddenly a brace of U. S. planes appeared, dropping flares and buzzing her bow. Quickly taking bearings, Eleanor exclaimed, "No wonder the Air Force is in a tizzy. We're in the restricted Eniwetok area!" Signaling her incapacity to do anything about it, she called the crew together, said quietly, "Let's sing a hymn." They had scarcely reached the third stanza when a freshening wind arose and, gaily waving to the distressed airmen, she wheeled the ship and set a direct course for Ponape.

Little by little she got the crew to teach her their own ancient sailing lore. This knowledge, handed down for hundreds of years by their ancestors, who had navigated frail outrigger canoes across thousands of miles of open sea, enabled her men to plot a course by wave patterns, cloud formations, the flight of birds.

One evening, arriving at an island too late to get into the pass, she gave orders to shorten sail, keep the ship on a slow course parallel to the reef. In the middle of the night, feeling vaguely uneasy, she went on deck to find her helmsman fast asleep, the wheel lashed, the *Star* drifting toward the reef only a few yards away. Swiftly, without disturbing the sleeper, she unlashed the helm and steered the ship out of danger. When the new watch appeared two hours later, she refused to turn over the wheel, manning it herself till daylight. None of the ashamed crewmen has ever again been caught asleep on duty.

Skippering the *Morning Star* entails not only sailing prowess but widely varied pastoral services ashore. Any visit to one of the hundreds of islands comprising Miss Wilson's 500,000-square-mile parish plunges her into a round of church services, marriages, funerals, christenings, plus conferences with the native pastor (who often is also the island chief) and teachers in the mission school.

The *Star's* visit is a long-anticipated event. When we arrived at Kili, the lovely little island to which the Bikini people had been transplanted by the U. S. government, a holiday was declared. The people flocked out from shore in their outriggers, led by King Judah, the chief. Ashore we were seated in a large thatch-roofed auditorium, leis thrown about our necks. Then, lustily singing a Marshallese welcome song, the islanders placed gifts before us—baskets full of rare shells, intricately woven hats and purses, great bunches of bananas, breadfruit, pandanus, taro, roast chickens. Gravely Judah told me: "We are very happy here. Please convey our thanks to America."

Since transportation through these immense watery reaches is virtually nonexistent save by outrigger canoe, the *Morning Star* has been for years the islanders' favorite means of getting about. No charge for passage is made. The itinerants bring their own food and sleep on deck amid great mounds of duffel. Says Miss Wilson, "They consider it *their* ship— and of course they're right. The *Star* can take 20 people, plus five tons of freight; it's first come, first carried." On one stretch between island stops we made, the *Star's* deck resembled nothing so much as the colonel's jeep in *Teahouse of the August Moon*.

Life aboard the *Morning Star* is, let us say, spiritually aseptic. Historically the islanders have considered their vessel a holy bark, freely at the service of all willing to comport themselves as in a church. But not for the unrestrained. In 1889, Robert Louis Stevenson and some bibulous companions requested passage from Honolulu to Micronesia on the *Morning Star IV;* informed of the rules, they hastily canceled the request.

The *Star's* crew, made up from members of the Marshallese Church, is like no other on any ship or any sea. Membership in the church—a self-governing, self-supporting body which makes its own stringent rules—is no frivolous matter. While most islanders are baptized Christians and regular attendants at church, membership is permitted only to those who do not smoke, drink, dance or trifle with the seventh commandment. No exceptions are made. Recently a king of Majuro Island was expelled for smoking, and got back in only after public confession and a promise to mend his ways.

Aboard, prayers and services are conducted twice daily. The men break into hymn-singing spontaneously—hymns heavy with assurance of God's care. When they lift their harmonious voices in *"Ta iman i jaje kio, bwelen dreka wor ak lan"* (Unknown waves before me roll, hiding rock and treacherous shoal) you know they are singing of deep, familiar reality, not poetic symbolism.

Between voyages, Eleanor Wilson supervises the church's intermediate boarding school at Jabwor, on Jaluit Atoll, and also does some teaching. In whatever spare time is left, she guides her students' recreation and reading, encourages them to think for themselves, ask questions, even challenge her precepts. "Don't just accept what I say," she needles them. "He who has never sincerely doubted has never truly learned!"

When on trips she often takes along her ninth-graders and holds classes on board, using these sea junkets to teach them about the outer world. Dr. Robert Gibson, director of education for the U.S. Trust Territory, told me: "Of all the dedicated and inspiring teachers I've seen in action anywhere, Eleanor Wilson tops them all."

Throughout the busy district centers of the Trust Terri-

tory, occupying positions of high importance to Micronesia's
future, I found scores of brilliant young Marshallese who had
studied under her during her pre-skipper days—at Kusaie,
Jaluit, Rong Rong, Majuro.

One is Kejeje, manager of the Jaluit branch of KITCO
(Kwajalein Island Trading Company), one of several native-
owned companies set up by the Trust Territory to supply
islanders with needed goods as well as teach them the practical benefits of capitalism. Kejeje told me how, while her
student at Rong Rong after World War II, he had been fired
with ambition by Miss Wilson's repeated challenge, "Some
day your people will have a chance to rule themselves. You
must be ready!"

Another is Dwight Heine, descendant of a German father
and a Marshallese mother, who under the Trust Territory
now directs all education projects in the Marshalls—the only
Micronesian to hold such a position. "The years I spent under
Miss Wilson's teaching," Heine asserts, "were the most important of my life. She taught me far more than academic
subjects. At first I watched her, suspicious. Why, I asked
myself, was so lovely a person devoting herself to a people
not of her own race? Through her I came to know that there
are individuals and nations who give themselves selflessly
to others, not for what they can get out of us but for what
they can put into us!"

Miss Wilson spent the war years in the United States, lecturing about the people on the unknown specks of coral
then being thrust into the headlines. With an aching heart
she read of the bombings of the islands she knew so well.
She wept upon hearing how her Marshallese had replied
when asked what they wanted and needed most. To

astounded U.S. Military poll-takers, with pencils poised to note down demands for creature comforts and doo-dads, the people said simply, "Just send us back our missionaries."

The war over, she was the first missionary back in the islands. Her post-war years were filled with rebuilding bombed-out mission schools and churches, rounding up students who had been for four years without education, hitching rides on Navy planes and ships to visit outer islands, comforting and reassuring the scattered and war-bewildered islanders.

She found herself spending much time explaining her fellow Americans to her adopted people, and vice versa. The latter problem took on some proportions one day when an overheated Navy officer barged into her quarters. "Did you advise the mothers of Marshallese girls not to let them attend Navy dances?" he demanded. Hinting that interference with the official program for Navy recreation was pretty close to high treason, he blustered that he had half a mind and all the power to "have you sent home!" Recovering, Eleanor Wilson smiled and said, "In that case, maybe I'd better see the Commodore—perhaps to say good-by?"

When, some days later, the base commander and his wife dropped in at her place for a social call, she told the story. "I did remind the mothers that if they did not wish their daughters to face the discipline of their own churches, they had better keep them from the Navy or any other dances. One must understand, Commodore, that the rules of the churches out here are much more severe than ours at home. They are not my rules, nor the rules of the Congregational-Christian Church of which I am a minister. But they govern the lives of these people. My advice was based not on my

personal opinion of dancing but on the desire to avoid
trouble for these young women.

"I certainly do not wish, sir, to make your problem of finding suitable recreation more difficult than it already is in
these islands. But the stay of your young men here is short.
The girls must go on living here, where church standing is
very important. Any girl who loses her membership might
find it impossible to marry well. I'm sure you'll agree, Commodore, that such things make for great difficulties not only
for missionaries but for the Navy."

The Commodore did agree, and the matter closed happily—for all but the frustrated officer. He, not Eleanor, was
"replaced" in the islands.

She and the Navy thenceforth got along famously. At mission stations where she taught school, most of them adjacent
to U.S. installations, she kept "open house" for Navy men,
baked them cookies and pies, planned parties aship and
ashore, counseled them in love problems, comforted the
homesick. In return, sailors voted her "the girl we most
couldn't get along without," took her picture, hung it up in
pinup spots, wangled for her rations of food and clothing,
abandoned building materials, transportation when she
needed it.

Once, on an otherwise womanless cruiser taking her to
Kwajalein, an officer gave her his cabin and the seamen
plastered a nearby "head" with her name, followed by
hers, proclaiming this her facility and no other's.

And when she got her ship, they declared, "You're in the
Navy now—one of us!"

In mid-1951, sorely in need of a furlough, she left her ship
in the hands of a Canadian missionary captain serving in

Eleanor Wilson, *Morning Star* skipper, teaching navigation to young Micronesians serving as members of her crew. (Chapter III)

Miss Wilson bicycling across her ship's island base at Majuro in the Marshall Islands.

Charles Péan, dauntless Salvation Army officer, shortly after arriving in French Guiana determined to abolish the "dry guillotine." (Chapter IV)

A *libéré* in Cayenne, French Guiana, one of 2500 "graduates" from Devil's Island whom Péan and his Salvationists helped rehabilitate through Christian compassion.

French convicts working in the broiling sun at Devil's Island, infamous French penal colony.

Okinawa and took a long-overdue leave. Some months later she received jolting news: the *Star* had foundered in a storm. She was now a skipper without a ship.

Then one day a friend found an adequate ship available in Japan for $17,000; she decided to put her need before the churches. Telling her story across the United States, she recounted how in 1904, she, as a youngster along with thousands of other children, had been one of the owners of the *Morning Star V.* "Little did I dream as I clutched my ten-cent share certificate," she told her audiences, "that I'd one day be a *Star* skipper!" She raised $20,000, much of it from the piggy banks of Sunday-school children who gave just as she had done.

In five months she was back in the Marshalls, where she and the new *Star* were wildly welcomed by singing islanders. At the U.S. Navy base on Kwajalein the commanding officer insisted on a proper christening of the vessel. Island women gaily festooned the *Star's* rigging with colorful strips of cloth; a huge lei of fragrant flowers was flung over the bow, another around the lady skipper's neck. Then, with solemn ceremony, a bottle of coconut juice was smashed against the bow.

As a fitting climax, before the little ship moved out, the voices of 400 islanders, joined by officers and men of the U.S. Navy, broke into a hymn sung at every *Star* christening for the past 100 years: "Waft, waft, ye winds, His story."

IV

The Man Who Conquered Devil's Island

After nearly a century, during which Devil's Island became synonymous with everything evil in penological inhumanity, France's notorious prison colony in French Guiana was being liquidated in 1946. And the man chosen by the French Government to smash the infamous "dry guillotine" —which, since its establishment in 1852, claimed more than 70,000 victims—was neither a government official nor a professional penologist. He was a mild-mannered little Salvation Army officer, Charles Péan.

Behind this choice lay a dramatic personal triumph—a triumph resulting from 18 years of unremitting labor on behalf of Devil's Islanders and an unfaltering faith that religion can transform human life on its most hopeless, most vicious, most degenerate levels.

The story of Péan's triumph is to me one of the great dramas of recent history, as well as a remarkable record of personal dedication and self-sacrifice.

Just after World War I, while a student at the University of Paris, Charles Péan came in contact with the Salvation Army's work. The Salvationists' motto—a man may be down but he is never out—fired his imagination.

70

Young Péan decided to give this theory a whirl. Switching from the social sciences to theology, he emerged from the university with a degree in divinity and placed his life at the disposal of the Salvation Army.

Péan was working in Paris' Montmartre when a newspaper printed a series of articles on conditions in the French Guiana penal settlement. It was not the first exposé. Periodically the world had been set back on its heels by reports from escaped convicts or visiting newspaper men. But each time public opinion had blown hot, then cold, then ceased to blow at all. This time the stirring was supplied by a French journalist, Albert Londres, and his exposures shocked public opinion as it had not been shocked since the Dreyfus case and Emile Zola's *J'Accuse*. Yet, like others before it, the fierce public demand for reform of Devil's Island flared only briefly then died down.

But it didn't die down in Charles Péan. Shocked and angry, he dug into libraries for previous accounts. He found himself longing to help these "incorrigibles." And something like the Apostle Paul's Macedonian call seemed to come to him from the faraway shores of Guiana. He had dedicated his life to the proposition that the "farthest down" could be lifted. Why not apply it to the pariahs of Devil's Island?

Penologists laughed at him, showed him records of a hundred attempts at Guiana reform—and a hundred failures. Péan was stubborn. "Perhaps all you say is true," he insisted. "But I'd like to see for myself." He wore down the authorities with his persistence. They gave him *carte blanche* to investigate as much as he liked, and shrugged him off. "You'll see," they said.

He did see. And he saw more and saw farther than the

officials in France had suspected. At Saint Laurent-du-Ma-
roni, the administrative center of the penal colony, he passed
through gates bearing the proud legend of the homeland,
"Liberty, Fraternity, Equality." It was the last he saw of
these principles in this crucified colony of crucified men.

For three months he poked about the colony. The officials
wanted to give him a "guided tour," but he insisted on striking out for himself, living with the prisoners, talking with
them, learning their ways of life—and death. He went into
steaming jungle labor camps where men newly come from
the temperate European climate worked naked and half-
starved in swampland swarming with mosquitoes and snakes,
and where sooner or later fever and dysentery got nearly
every man. He spent nights in blockhouses where 30 to 40
convicts were locked in each cramped and stifling compart-
ment, and visited the disciplinary barracks where men became maniacal after months of solitary confinement. He
discovered that of the 1000 or more prisoners sent out from
France yearly less than one tenth lived as long as five
years.

He spent days at infamous Camp Saint-Jean, the "dead
end" of the settlement, home of those who had been banished
for life to the colony. Here men, chained like wild beasts or
herded together in immoral squalor, were kept in cells and
blockhouses with the syphilitic, the cancerous, the leprous,
the tubercular.

But it was the colony's 2500 *libérés* who struck Péan as
the most pitiful wretches of all. Although these men had
served their terms as convicts, they were required, under
France's infamous law of *doublage*, to remain in the colony
for a period equal to their sentence if it were less than eight

years, or for life if their sentence ran more than eight years. Moreover, they had to provide their own passage money home. Because there was no way by which a man could earn more than a few francs, almost any sentence to Devil's Island was for life.

As convicts, they had at least been lodged, fed and clothed. As *libérés*, they wandered around the shoddy towns of Saint-Laurent and Cayenne in tattered rags, their beards and hair uncut for weeks, their faces gaunt, desperately hunting for scraps to eat. There was a saying current among the *libérés*: "When freedom is gained, then your sentence begins."

Nearly all tried to escape. Few got away from the colony; of those who did, only a handful were ever heard from again. Sharks, quicksands or starvation in the jungles claimed the rest.

Péan found that in all the colony there was no chaplain, minister, priest, or even a chapel to bring the consolations of religion to these neediest of all men.

He also discovered that the officials took an airy attitude toward reform of any kind. When Prince Napoleon established the colony in 1852, one of his ministers asked, "By whom will you have the convicts guarded?" The Prince replied, "By worse crooks than they are." That set the pattern, and it obtained, with few exceptions, throughout. Many a well-meaning governor went to French Guiana for his two-year term with big plans and high hopes. But the permanent Penal Administration officials there had him beaten before he started. They would trump up charges to have him recalled, thereby putting a blot on his political career, or undermine his plans through inertia and delay, knowing he would

be transferred after two years while they—and their graft—
went on forever.

But now, hot with anger at all he had seen, Péan went to
the current governor of the colony. "It seems impossible in
this 20th century," he stormed, "that France has more than
400 employes engaged in a penal service the only result of
which is the complete physical and moral degradation of
6000 men!"

The governor sighed. "I agree with you, Captain. But it's
no use. This is a little hell no man can conquer." He smiled
wearily. "Perhaps it's even too big a job for God!"

"That, Your Excellency," replied Péan, "remains to be
seen."

He returned to France burning not only with anger but
with tropical fever. For 18 months he was bedridden, and in
his delirious nights the gaunt, hopeless faces of the *libérés*
haunted him. Finally he arose shakily from his sickbed to
push his crusade. He drew up a two-part program: first, a
long-range plan to abolish the settlement; pending that, a
moral and social reformation plan for the convicts and
libérés. He wrote articles, spoke at innumerable meetings
throughout France, haunted official chambers, kept the name
Devil's Island ablaze in the conscience of government.

It took Péan three and a half years to win the backing of
the Ministry of Justice. Then, in 1933, he sailed again for
French Guiana, this time with three other Salvation Army
officers. The penal officials at Saint-Laurent greeted his return with little enthusiasm. But since he had the backing of
the Ministry of Justice they gave him their indifferent support. After all, they reasoned, he could do little harm—and
perhaps his plan for helping the *libérés* would take some

worry off their minds. He wangled the use of an abandoned building and picked workers from the *libérés* to renovate the place and to act as cooks and helpers in the dining room and dormitories. One *libéré*, a former Left Bank artist who had slain his mistress, painted a sign: "L'Armée Salut—Le Foyer" (The Salvation Army Home), adding with a flourish "The House of Hope."

The shelter's inaugural was ill-starred. Péan had planned to celebrate the opening with a free meal for all comers. But when it was time to eat, he discovered that his cooks and waiters had found some wine and gone off on a spree. The four Salvationists, their faces red, flung off their tunics and served the meal to 2000 famished guests—while the penal officials present smiled knowingly. That night some of the "guests" returned and stole the cutlery and china, most of the provisions, the workshop tools, and even the cords from the flagstaff!

Undaunted, Péan and his officers began anew. It took two months to replace the stolen materials and get the restaurant in working order again. Then they started other projects. They opened a second home for *libérés* in Cayenne. In the jungle they developed a farm to raise vegetables and meat for cafeterias. Carpenter shops were set up to turn out furniture for the shelters and carved objects for sale abroad. Out of virgin jungle Péan and a half-dozen *libérés* hewed a banana plantation which was to supply work for the men and profit for the homes. "There is work for every man who wants to earn his keep," said Péan, and even among these hardened and cynical prisoners he found enough help to carry on.

The difficulties were all but insuperable. The colony's

"merchants" who acted as receivers for stolen goods, the peddlers of a cheap brand of rum called "tafia," the native women, the corrupt prison guards—all saw in the Salvationists a threat to their racket. Anonymous threats invited them to leave the colony—or else. Clever traps were set to discredit them. They were waylaid at night by assailants, and once Péan's assistant's jaw was broken. Civil magistrates and police gave little protection; some even connived with convicts and *libérés* to rid the colony of these "do-gooders."

Friendly officers of the penal colony shook their heads at Péan's methods of building the felons' faith in him and in themselves. An embezzler was put in charge of the accounts; a man who had served time for poisoning his wife was made cook in one of the shelters; a rapist-killer guarded the home of a Salvation Army officer while he was away and his wife was alone. But to the *libérés* the strange tonic of being trusted proved morally invigorating.

Only one failed monumentally, and his remorse drove him, like Judas, to commit suicide. This fellow, Guillon by name, Péan had fished out of the moral cesspool at the Saint-Jean camp, and appointed him accountant at the Saint-Laurent shelter. After months of sobriety and apparent rectitude of life, Guillon suddenly resigned his job, went to live with a Negress, and stayed drunk most of the time—something dark in his immediate past driving him frantic. He showed up one night at the shelter, implored Péan to forgive him, and fled sobbing. The next morning his body was found hanging from the beams in the Negress' home. On his desk were copies of notes he had made daily during his service with Péan, notes that recorded every action of the Salvationists which he had supplied to certain elements in the colony who were trying to pin something on them. His traitorous act had preyed upon his mind, and he had made the traitor's atonement.

Religious services were held in the jungle camps and blockhouses, and for the *libérés*. But religion was forced down no man's throat. All Péan asked was an honest effort at self-saving. And slowly a few converts were made. Péan gave them bits of colored ribbon to wear as a steady reminder of the new life they had espoused.

In time the farms, plantations, workshops and shelters were financially solvent. Sales of convict-manufactured items abroad, plus the royalties from the books Péan wrote on life in the colony, supplied Péan with the funds for his long-dreamed-of program to repatriate *libérés* who had served their *doublage*.

Péan's plan was designed not only to get the *libérés* home but to restore their strength of character so that they would become good citizens.

Péan called his plan "The New Doublage." When a *libéré* applied for work, he was told that for his labor he would receive lodging, meals and two francs a day. At the end of each month he would also receive a coupon worth 40 francs. He could exchange this coupon for ready money. But if he saved 20 coupons, and thus had 800 francs to his credit, he would get in exchange a ticket to France costing 1600 francs. Moreover, the Salvation Army would meet him at the docks in France and sponsor his new start in life.

This was a boon not only to the short-termers but also to those condemned to perpetual exile—for Péan had dug up an almost forgotten provision in the law governing *doublage* which stated that any *libéré* who maintained himself for five years after release from convict status, without having attempted escape or otherwise incurred punishment, was eligible to leave the colony. Under the old conditions, this provision was an empty one, for it had been virtually impossible either to pile up five years' good conduct, to earn a living, or to resist escape.

The relatively few who had been able to get back to France had made sorry records. Their moral nature vitiated by long residence in such a place and among such compatriots, they were no match for the odds against them in the homeland. With no better papers than those stamped with the Penal Administration insignia, employment was almost impossible to obtain, and they quickly drifted back into crime.

Péan's scheme—if it worked—would change all that. Surprisingly, it did work!

To men whose every waking thought was of fleeing Guiana, the plan offered a huge incentive. Less than two years after "The New Doublage" was instituted, the first crop of *libérés* sailed for France. Péan sailed with them. "The whole future of your comrades in Guiana, and of the colony itself," he kept reminding them, "depends on you." Newsmen met their ship, and editorials the next day predicted an immediate crime wave from "Péan's Pariahs." The crime wave failed to develop—then or later. Péan's pariahs came back rehabilitated not only socially but spiritually. By 1939 he had returned 804 convicts—and only three were ever in trouble with the police again.

Meanwhile Péan divided his time between Guiana and France, continuing his fight to have the colony abolished. He was now recognized as an expert on Devil's Island. He had accomplished—not in just a few cases but in wholesale lots, and on the toughest of material—the thing penologists and social scientists had said was impossible. When a commission was appointed to draft a law to liquidate the colony, he was the only nongovernment member.

He did not rest here. He knew that the feet of any wide-reaching reform move slowly, and that many a measure dies within reach of its goal simply because those pushing it stop too soon. A half dozen times before, reforms affecting the colony had been voted by the Chamber of Deputies only to be defeated in the Senate. And each time reports had gone out to the world that Devil's Island was to be abolished. Even while the proposed law was being drafted, Péan kept up his pressure. He blew the trumpets everywhere. The Salvation Army arranged mass meetings in Paris and other cities, inviting leading members of government to speak, putting them on the spot.

In 1938 the President of France signed a decree forbidding sentences to Devil's Island and substituting penal servitude in a standard penitentiary. Convicts already in Guiana were to stay there until their sentences were served, but then they could leave. The colony, it was thought, would be gradually depopulated during the next ten years.

The war interrupted Péan's work; he was trapped in France by the German invaders. Unknown to him, however, the De Gaulle government-in-exile put most of his ideas into effect. And early in 1946 came the official order to liquidate the colony.

Péan was the government's unanimous choice to supervise the liquidation. With his commission in his pocket, "the happiest document I ever carried," he arrived at Saint-Laurent on Good Friday. Nobody had known of his coming, but the news spread quickly. Convicts and *libérés* came from miles around to spread flowers in his path and welcome him like a conquering hero. Péan was so moved that tears rolled down his cheeks.

On Easter Sunday a mass meeting was held in his honor. From a rude platform Péan looked out over the great crowd of men for whose saving he had given 18 years of his life. On his breast was pinned the ribbon of an Officer of the Legion of Honor. The closing words of the citation that went with it read: *"He has the soul of an apostle."*

But when he attempted to speak to the crowd he had no apostolic message. All he could murmur was: "How fitting that this meeting should be held on Easter Sunday!"

His voice broke, and he got no further. But it was enough. His pariahs understood.

V

The Miracle of the "Omi Brotherhood"

On a chill February day back in 1905 a young American, fired with an offbeat concept of missionary service, stepped from a rattletrap train at a remote village in rural Japan, plopped his satchel down on the deserted platform, and was swept momentarily with a sense of his own folly. Backed by no church or mission board, he had abandoned a promising career as an architect to take a post as English teacher at a commercial academy.

He shucked off his misgivings by reminding himself of the two-pronged point he had come 7000 miles to prove: (1) that Christianity always makes a far bigger impact "where it is talked the least, lived the most," and (2) that a self-supporting layman could demonstrate religion's practical application to society far more effectively than could any clergyman.

Having spent his last borrowed dollar to get here, understanding not a word of the Japanese language, he scarcely knew how he would go about proving his point. But, given a spirit of utter dedication, he was sure a means could be found . . .

Today, more than a half century later, the name and fame

of William Merrell Vories is known throughout the Far East. Toyohiko Kagawa has called him "Japan's greatest Christian." And the "Omi Brotherhood" he founded has been heralded by such American religious leaders as Dr. Glenn Clark as "the most remarkable missionary adventure of modern times."

Tools of the Omi Brotherhood, in which more than 1000 Japanese Christians live and work communally, are not pulpits and churches but factories and schools. It owns properties valued at $1,700,000, conducts commercial enterprises grossing more than a million dollars annually; and its architectural department, busiest in all Japan, has designed and built some 2800 buildings.

Yet the Brotherhood is a community where nobody works for personal profit; where everyone, from top managerial brains to humblest laborer, exerts himself according to his best ability and is paid only according to his barest needs —for one purpose: to demonstrate that Christian principles are as workable in daily life as they are decorative to Sunday creed.

From Vories' zeal (and Brotherhood profits from its commercial enterprises) have come, among other things: one of the most progressive school systems in the Far East; a large TB sanatorium, finest and most modern in Japan; a YMCA through which pass thousands of boys and men annually; an evangelistic department that has founded 13 churches, supports scores of ministers and full-time workers serving 23 other preaching places and 36 Sunday schools involving 2500 pupils, and runs a unique "Find Christ by Mail" project that reaches into virtually every home in Japan.

In Omi-Hachiman recently, I was shown through this

amazing community by Merrell Vories himself. A wispy little man with the poundage of a jockey and the mystical drive of a saint, he modestly told me how his dream had mushroomed.

Born into a devout family that often entertained missionaries on home leave, Vories contracted in his teens "a vague itch to sashay off to far places and save the world." He kept the irritation under control, however, by developing a counter-itch for architecture. Attending Colorado College, he sidestepped the challenges of Student Volunteer Movement recruiters by saying, "I'm going to be an architect, make a lot of money; then I can support a half dozen missionaries."

But before his graduation he recognized this for what it was: a dodge. When he heard of the martyrdom of Chinese Christians during the Boxer uprising, then raging, an accusing voice seemed to say, "They willingly give their heads for their faith; you're not willing to give up even your ambitions!"

That did it. He would be a missionary—but not in the usual mold. He felt no call to the ministry. Like Socrates the stone-cutter, or Paul the tent-maker, he would support himself by some convenient vocation, make evangelism his avocation. To friends he said, "If I can only find some spot too inconspicuous to appeal to any other missionary, I'll go to the ends of the earth!"

He almost did. Learning through the International YMCA that a teacher of English was wanted by a town deep in Japan's hinterland named Omi-Hachiman, he told his family, "It's come, my dream job!" And borrowing $250 from his father for a one-way passage to Japan, he set out.

In Tokyo he was warned, "You're going to a stronghold of

fanatical Buddhism, whose priests won't look with benevolence on any Christian proselytizing you hope to do. But it's virgin soil; you'll have three-quarters of a million people all to yourself!"

Arrived at Omi-Hachiman after a 17-hour train ride, he trudged off to the house set aside for him—a 300-year-old shack that had quartered a swift succession of his predecessors. That first night an earthquake rattled its boards, and shivering alone in the bare, nine-room structure, he wrote in his diary, "Homesick, cold, lonely. *But here!*"

His loneliness melted fast when, three days later, he began classes at the academy. Intrigued by having a "genuine American" in their midst, his students tagged him around after class, followed him home. He invited them to make his house their rendezvous, introduced them to dominoes and Flinch, spent all his salary on refreshments for his guests.

After a few days, he announced the start of Bible study, expecting a half dozen; 45 showed up for the first class. Within a few weeks he had four groups going, with 322 enrolled. If Bible study palled, his blackboard could be flipped over to become a Ping-pong table.

When several of the boys became Christians, Vories invited them to come live with him, sharing expenses. Soon his "family" included eight of the academy's leaders, with others begging to get in.

With his house bursting at the seams with eager youngsters, Vories knew he had to expand. Why not open a YMCA? A letter to 30 friends in America brought enough to start; a successful dairyman in Kyoto, a native of Omi who had become a Christian, contributed a choice lot. Soon Vories had his student center under construction, with dormitory space for converts and adequate rooms for Bible study and recreation.

Buddhist priests, alarmed, incited school roughnecks to dragoon the rival faith. Boys known to be attending the Bible classes were lampooned, assaulted with baseball bats, pushed into the canal. But when Vories advised his boys to take their persecution in good grace, to pray for their persecutors, the fight went out of the bullies; intrigued, several became converts themselves.

The priests then instituted a vicious drive to get Vories dismissed from his teaching post, pressuring the province's leading newspaper to run a series of articles denouncing Christianity—and Vories. Their campaign succeeded. At the end of his second year at the academy, the axe fell: his contract was not renewed.

Out of a job, Vories took stock of his situation. Everything he'd earned had gone into the YMCA building. Before the whole province he was branded a pernicious influence. Bleakly he reflected that not even Job had been more thoroughly stripped and left sitting in the ashes of his hopes.

But when he remembered how his boys had stood up under persecution, saw them now waiting loyally to join his next move, he rebounded with zest. One of his first converts offered to share his living allowance, 17 yen ($8.50) per month; others contributed as they were able. Vories himself managed to get odd jobs tutoring; at nights he laid out the format of a little publication he named "The Mustard Seed," sent it to American friends inviting subscriptions. The magazine's first issue graphically described his new building, enthusiastically stated his hopes and dreams. It contained no mention of his dismissal ("I didn't want to begin with bad news!"). Many promptly subscribed at $1 a year, providing enough dollars to stave off disaster.

Then one night, while sleeplessly pondering how he might further undergird his wobbly mission, the thought came: Why not put his knowledge of architecture to work? Taking this night-blooming notion to be the voice of God, he leapt out of bed to awaken his associates, saying, "We'll form an architectural firm!"

The next morning he cleared a space in the dormitory, dug out an old set of drawing instruments he'd brought along, rigged up a drawing table, started classes in drafting, and announced grandly that the new architectural firm of "W. M. Vories & Co." was in business.

To the objection that there was little future for a firm centered in an unknown country town, he replied, "The most remote place, if it be the place where God has placed us, offers ample field for the best we possess."

His first student-draftsman was a convert from one of the early Bible classes. Following Vories' use of the beatitude "Blessed are the pure in heart" as an introductory to a slashing attack on local prostitution, the boy had risen to wistfully ask, "Teacher, how can I become a pure man?" It was a good question: he lived in a notorious brothel owned by his uncle, was being trained to take over as manager. Vories had brought him to his house to live; he later became one of the Brotherhood's founders.

The firm's start coincided, happily, with a rising boom in Western-style buildings. In earthquaky Japan, Vories learned to build so as to absorb the shocks; soon he was erecting structures that stood while others toppled, in time grappling with more orders than he could handle.

In later years, after his firm was doing more business than any other in Japan, he would recall, "With reluctance I'd abandoned my dream of becoming an architect, feeling I'd wasted all those years of study. Isn't that just like God? He asks us to give up a selfish ambition, then gives it back to us, saying, 'Use it for My sake!'"

Vories and his growing group of co-workers agreed to live co-operatively, pooling their resources, sharing equally all responsibility, taking from their earnings only bare living expenses, turning back all the rest into evangelism. Evenings and week-ends they left their drawing boards for villages crowding the shores of 40-mile-long Lake Biwa, setting up Sunday schools and Bible classes which grew into churches. To supply the new churches with leadership, promising young converts were sent off to seminaries to be trained as pastors.

Until Vories came to Omi Province (now Shiga Prefecture) there was not in all its 1616 square miles a single permanent Christian church. Before long he had several congregations going full tilt, each with its own building and pastor.

Growth was so rapid that shortly Vories was sighing, "We planned to advance on our knees; we seem to be racing on our tiptoes!"

Pattern for all others was the church in Omi-Hachiman, established in Vories' third year. From the first he insisted that it be self-supporting, indigenously led. Even plate collections were abolished when, one Sunday while playing the offertory on the organ, he noted in a mirror the embarrassment of some worshipers too poor to give. To the church committee he said, "Making people give because they are ashamed to be seen not giving is not good." Thereafter all church expenses were met by secret but systematic pledges by members.

Meanwhile, Vories used his architectural services for "evangelizing" of another sort. To all clients he made it clear that "Christian principles will be applied to every job from drawing board to completed structure," and that such principles ruled out all "bribes, commissions, gifts." Aghast, members of Japan's traditionally graft-ridden building trades debated among themselves whether he was crazy or just crafty.

One holding the latter belief discovered his mistake when Vories sought bids for a large school he had designed. A few hours before the sealed bids were to be opened, this bidder dropped by to say coyly, "If I get the job there will be 100,000 yen ($50,000) in it for you." Flushing with anger, Vories thrust the sealed envelopes toward him, saying, "Find yours, and take it back. You've eliminated yourself!"

Early clients were equally aghast to learn that Vories' "Christian principles" called for no Sunday work and a 44-hour week. He argued—and proved—that a man does better work, and more of it, when he has time off to spend with his family.

One to whom he proved it was the president of a large Osaka bank for whom he had designed a $2 million building. Learning that Vories was imposing his 8-hour day, no-Sunday-work rule, the banker stormed: "We'll be delayed for weeks getting in. Do you realize what that will cost us in interest—to say nothing in prestige?" Vories only shrugged, "I'll retire in favor of another firm if you like." Impatiently the banker replied, "I'm only asking you to make an exception in our case." To which Vories rejoined, smiling, "If I compromise now on what I know is a sound principle, compromising might get to be a habit; I might even find myself taking a few extra thousands in graft from the contractor!" The banker gave up; the building was finished weeks ahead of the contract deadline.

Vories exulted, "We're building more than buildings!"

By 1948 his architectural firm had established branch offices in Osaka, Tokyo, Seoul, Mukden, Peking.

Among the 2800 buildings he has constructed are some of the largest and most modern in Japan. A sample is the famous Daimaru department store in Osaka, occupying a square block and costing more than $10 million. Its owner, having visited in America and England, returned to tell Vories, "Build me the biggest and most lavish store in the world." Vories did. Another monument to his handiwork is the new International Christian University in Tokyo.

In 1909 he formed the Omi Sales Co., Ltd., a firm for importing building materials not available in Japan. He quickly expanded the firm's scope when, in America the following year to make business contacts, he met A. A. Hyde, founder of the Mentholatum Company. Fascinated, Hyde listened to his story, then said, "You say you need some bigger industry to supply jobs for converts. Why not distribute my product? You can have the exclusive rights—and the profits."

Hurrying back to Japan with a few cases of Mentholatum, Vories ran head-on into the pharmaceutical combine. When druggists refused to stock the product, he talked Christian organizations into selling it, gave them the profits. When demand became brisk, druggists came begging. By 1930 sales were so huge that Hyde suggested, "Why not make Mentholatum as well as distribute it? You furnish the building, I'll furnish the machinery and the formula."

Vories designed a model factory, hired hundreds of workers, plunged into wholesale production, and eventually some 30,000 stores were selling eight millon packages a year.

With the adding of more departments and more worker-converts, Vories knew he must give form as well as spirit to his Omi mission. But what form? He wanted no transcendental colony or monastic retreat, but a community that would be "a practical demonstration of Christianized economics working in the world today." To remove any suggestion of foreign control or denominational bias, one of his first acts was to change the name from "mission" to Brotherhood.

The form he adopted was virtually what it is today. Membership in the Brotherhood is limited to the number of workers needed in the various departments—evangelistic, industrial, educational—and open only to those willing to subscribe to its aims and ideals. Whatever one's job, as top executive or common laborer, his wages are according to his living needs, no more, no less. The average Brotherhood wage is $62 a month. For emergencies the Brotherhood provides from its common treasury. All policies and decisions are made by a 12-man Executive Committee, whose members are elected for two-year terms, act as chairmen of the ruling body in alphabetical rotation, report its actions and decisions to the Brotherhood's monthly meeting.

To conform to Japanese law, three different forms of incorporation were necessary: one each for the strictly religious and philanthropic activities, the industrial department, the architectural section. All earnings, however, go into a common treasury which dispenses departmental appropriations as needed.

Close-knit as are the members, they do not live in clannish solitude from their Omi neighbors. Only a few families own or rent homes in the compound. Vories made no rules against ownership of property, though he himself never wanted to. When, on his 70th birthday, the Brotherhood planned to build a home for him, he stopped them saying, "You can't build for everyone. I don't want anything that any other member can't have."

Vories' paternal solicitude for his workers was revolutionary. When he came, Japan's switch from feudalism to the machine age had just begun. There were as yet no labor unions, no fair-wage laws. Workers were a commodity to be bought at the cheapest price, worked incredibly long hours, were discarded when exhausted.

Against the background of such evils Vories framed the Brotherhood's cardinal principles: "(1) Labor should be a part of any industrial organization, not just an outside commodity to be bought like raw materials; (2) excessive salaries to ornamental officials should be eliminated or drastically cut; (3) industry should concentrate on producing commodities that are needed, of good quality and at reasonable prices—with service to society as the prime goal."

The Brotherhood's plants have never known a walkout or strike. Member-workers are free to leave, through dissatisfaction or for higher pay, at any time. Few ever have.

When Communists came to Omi, foraging for discontent, they found little to work on, went away sourly saying, "The Brotherhood has beaten us to it."

To Vories the Brotherhood's astounding financial success

was gratifying, but incidental. He told his workers, "What we produce, in goods or profits, is not of prime importance. Most important is how and why we live and work as we do. The Brotherhood is not an argument for Christianity; it's a *demonstration.*"

He was a stickler for high standards of personal conduct. Only once did he have to crack down—in 1918, when four younger members of the Brotherhood were caught in a morality lapse. He dramatically announced that, as an act of public contrition, the entire Brotherhood was being dissolved for three days, with offices closed and all work suspended. It would be reestablished only when all members voluntarily returned "with a renewed pledge to the central purpose of the movement." The action made nationwide news, purged the Brotherhood once and for all, gave him a chance to express his thesis that "only an organization that stands ready to kill itself for the sake of its principles is qualified to live."

I walked through the Brotherhood's model factories and office buildings, situated on a beautifully landscaped 3-acre compound. Factory rooms are light and airy, equipped with modern machinery. Workers pursue tasks to soft music piped in, eat in a shiny cafeteria, purchase food and household needs at a large commissary Vories calls his "supermarket," relax on playgrounds and in indoor gyms and recreation rooms.

A happy religious atmosphere pervades the whole compound. Bible study rooms occupy every free space. Each day's work begins with a devotional service in a large chapel atop the main building. On the chapel's walls the factory motto enjoins all to "Make Today Better Than Yesterday," and prayer is offered "that we might perform our work as unto Thee."

In later years industrialists came from all over Japan to marvel at the factories' modern design, study its management. Many invited Vories to redesign their own plants, lecture their management on methods of making workers happier in their work. This gave him further chance to preach on Christian incentive which, he said, "disproves the ancient theory of economists that only the hope of personal gain can induce human beings to exert themselves in productive labor."

To visitors puzzled over the Brotherhood's success, Vories once said, "Either this is a work of God, demonstrating what can be accomplished by the least able of mortals responsive to His leading, or it is a preposterous combination of 'lucky chances' befalling a group of self-deluded cranks. Take your choice!"

A good example of how Vories made the Brotherhood's every enterprise carry its message is its "Mentholatum evangelism." Printed on every package is a note inviting inquiries about Christianity. More than 6000 came during the first year, resulting in the formation of a "correspondence course in the Christian faith." Enrollees among prisoners alone number up to 1200 at a time. Others taking the course pay only a small sum to help with the mailing costs; they may also participate in the Brotherhood's 3000-volume circulating library, paying only the return postage on books borrowed. Because of the thousands of converts thus made, Mentholatum is known in rural Japan as "the Jesus medicine." Few converts are "quickies"; one man studied the course for 30 years before becoming a Christian.

Today the Correspondence Evangelism Department employs a large staff including a dozen specially trained pastors. The department head, Jisaburo Yamamoto, has his own story of dramatic conversion through Vories' hound-of-heaven persistence.

Yamamoto was one of Vories' first Bible class members 50 years ago. Upon learning of the boy's conversion to Christianity, his father, a prominent dealer in *sake* (Japan's fiery drink made from fermented rice), demanded he come home, prepare to succeed him in the family business. Yamamoto left with Vories' angry words ringing in his ears: "If you told me you're too weak to resist, I'd understand. But when you tell me you're going to make your living making others miserable, we'll have to part company."

One day, 15 years later, Vories and some tourist friends were checking out of a seaside resort when the inn-keeper told him the hotel had been engaged for a convention of *sake*-makers. At the wharf, Vories was going through the gate to his ship when a horde of delegates debarked. At their head was Yamamoto. Red-faced, his former pupil stammered, "Teacher, forgive me. I must chair this convention, but when it's over, I will close down my *sake* business."

Stubbornly, Vories blocked the gate, created a scene, coldly said, "If you pass through this gate you will go to hell." When Yamamoto hesitated, he said, "Come with me; let's talk it over." Yamamoto spent most of the night with Vories; the next day, accompanied by Vories, he returned home to publicly announce a change of occupation. To a big public meeting called to inform his employees and townsmen, Yamamoto said simply, "I disgraced my old teacher. But he loved me so much he was willing to make a fool of himself to save me."

The TB sanatorium got its start when, one day in 1917, a TB-ridden Buddhist priest named Kanyru Endo suddenly appeared at Vories' door. Disgusted by the immorality of his fellow-priests, Endo-san had left his temple nearby, was wandering aimlessly near Omi-Hachiman when, pausing to rest at a roadside station erected by the Brotherhood for weary travelers, his curiosity had been aroused by a sign, "Come unto me all ye that are heavy laden, and I will give you rest."

The priest and Vories spent most of the night arguing heatedly the relative merits of their faiths. Finally Vories said, "This is pretty futile, isn't it? Tell you what, stay with us for six months. We'll both agree not to mention religion, much less try to convert each other. If your life demonstrates the superiority of your faith, I'll become a Buddhist. But if, on the other hand, you find our brand of Christianity has merit, well . . ."

The priest agreed, was given a light job in the drafting office. One day Endo-san rose in a Brotherhood prayer meeting to say, "I have found a real faith at last; may I be baptized?" A few months later, contracting pneumonia, he lay dying. His last request to Vories: "Why not start a sanatorium for TB patients? Even if you can't cure them, you can give them the peace I've found."

Acquiring a plot of land on a sunny hillside, Vories built the sanatorium's first unit early in 1918. Its first resident physician was an early convert who had left the community to go through the Imperial University, became a doctor, returned to serve the Brotherhood.

Today the sanatorium has 180 beds, 37 buildings covering several acres, treats hundreds of patients annually for only the cost of their food, is credited with sparking scores of similar institutions throughout Japan. To it come health authorities from all over the Far East, modeling their institutions on its architecture and methods of treating Japan's age-old killer.

The Brotherhood's progressive school system likewise arose out of an important event in Vories' life: his marriage in 1919. Called to Tokyo to design a residence for a nobleman, he soon found himself in love with his client's younger sister, Maki Hitotsuyanagi. Daughter of a *Daiymo*, feudal ruler of a large province, Maki had spent nine years in the States, was educated at Bryn Mawr College. Their marriage caused consternation among Japan's nobility. It was permitted only after 18 months of "negotiations" and final sanction of the Imperial Household.

The wedding ceremony was performed in a college chapel Vories had constructed; the reception held in the nobleman's residence he'd designed; the honeymoon spent in a mountain resort cottage he'd built for Omi workers. "Surely," he exclaimed happily, "no architect could ask for happier settings for the greatest event in his life!"

Vories brought his bride back to an Omi fearful of what the induction of this dainty daughter of the aristocracy might do to the humble Brotherhood. The members' worries lessened when Merrell and Maki went to live in the poorest of the OB's outstations, vanished entirely when she refused servants, insisting on doing her own housework in its tumbledown cottage.

With Maki in charge, Vories' long plans of an educational

system for his Brotherhood went into high gear. In short order she created a rash of playgrounds, nursery schools, kindergartens, night schools for workers. She also introduced high school courses within the OB's plants where, in five large classrooms, 120 girl employees work five hours, study three, are paid for eight.

Today, in a modern educational plant donated by Mrs. A. A. Hyde of Wichita, Kansas, 450 students from kindergarten through senior high school study under the most advanced pedagogical methods, taught entirely by 43 full-time Christian teachers. Object of the thriving educational program: "to train Christian leaders for the Japan of tomorrow."

By 1940 Vories had seen his Brotherhood zoom into national prominence, more than validating his most roseate vision. A large Tokyo newspaper named him "not only first citizen of Omi-Hachiman but among the first in all Japan."

But he got his biggest kick out of the complete switch of sentiment that had occurred in Omi-Hachiman itself. From the old academy that summarily dismissed him years before came repeated invitations to lecture—on Christian ethics. When in 1934 the academy needed public support to build a new plant, he was asked to head the list of subscribers. Knowing he had no money of his own, the Brotherhood subscribed $5000 for him, saying, "Now you've got revenge on those who fired you—a Christian revenge!"

Buddhists no longer picture Vories with horns and cloven hoofs. One of the last to surrender was a wealthy man named Nishikawa, owner of an expansive 300-year-old ancestral mansion in Omi. One day, hearing that Nishikawa was critically ill of diabetes, Vories rushed over with a supply of insulin, saved his life. Amazed, the crusty old Buddhist demanded,

"Why do you do this for me, your old enemy?" Vories smiled, "Were you? I didn't know." Before his death Nishikawa transferred his residence to the Brotherhood for use as a dormitory for students.

Vories was proudest of all that his Brotherhood succeeded in becoming self-supporting and self-directing. He bridled a bit when some missionaries, comfortably backed by home boards, wondered aloud whether his mission would not die with him. He replied, "The very question predicates the old mistaken idea of a mission. If it is to send out an endless line of sectarian foreigners to control and direct native workers, to live aloof from the people, and to dispense foreign money in perpetuity, then missions had better stay away."

As for the "permanency" of his life-work, he wrote with some asperity in his book *The Omi Brotherhood in Nippon:* "What if a mission is not permanent? We have no desire to perpetuate anything after its work is accomplished. On the other hand, if ours is a true brotherhood—indigenous, self-supporting, untainted with overlapping or compromising connections with classes and castes—its permanency should take care of itself."

Thus far it has.

In 1940 Vories applied for naturalization as a Japanese citizen. The process took seven months; in January 1941 he got his official papers. Eleven months later came Pearl Harbor, precipitating him into his deepest Gethsemane.

Though Omi-Hachiman was not bombed, the war took its toll. The Brotherhood's industries were retarded, its educational program disrupted, its religious activities hampered. Younger members were drafted, many killed. Only the armed forces' need for Mentholatum saved the factory from confiscation and the membership from dissolution. The TB sanatorium was taken over for a military hospital; the OB's presses, used for printing its flood of books and evangelical literature, were junked for scrap iron. The military clique, moving in to mobilize the community's resources, conscripted school children and older workers for labor in food production and war factories, prohibited use of the English language, ordered all citizens to bow before Shinto shrines.

When Vories objected, the military spread the suggestion that he was an American spy, started a whispering campaign that disturbed the prefectural governor and police officials, made the whole Brotherhood suspect. However, when the vicious rumor reached Tokyo the emperor promptly scotched it by sending his brother, Prince Tagamatsu, to Omi-Hachiman—the first time a member of the Imperial family had visited the prefecture. The governor heard the prince say of the Brotherhood, "This would be possible under any other auspices than Christianity," later became a Christian himself.

To prevent further suspicion from touching his Brotherhood, Vories accepted an offer from Tokyo and Kyoto universities to teach a course in advanced English started years before by Lafcadio Hearn. He found, to his delight, that the deans of both were Christians, and that most students in his crowded classes were unaffected by the jingoists, interested both in America and Christianity. He managed to make several converts among them, was vastly cheered to find that such evangelizing could be done "right in the midst of war."

Vories spent the last seven months of the war at Karuizawa, a mountain resort where the Brotherhood maintained an architectural office. Here food was scarce, and he and Maki were often forced to forage in the hills for edible leaves and weeds. But also at Karuizawa was the summer villa of the Crown Prince who, learning of their need, often shared his food with them. Vories, who never missed a chance to talk and pray with members of the royal family, finally succeeded in converting Prince Masohito, the emperor's second son.

The war's abrupt end brought Vories a rare opportunity to serve both his native and adopted lands. From Prince Konoe, former prime minister who had been ousted by the military clique, came a message: "Will you act as liaison between the new government and the American occupation authority?"

For the next several weeks Vories, a little man in a big black limousine, shuttled between the Imperial Palace and General MacArthur's headquarters, interpreting the conquered to the conquerors, helping turn a land long held in the brutal grip of military exploiters into a vital democracy.

Under MacArthur's benevolent reforms, strongly underscored with religious faith, Vories found the Japanese clamorous to learn more about Christianity. An avalanche of invitations implored him to lecture in colleges, conduct evangelistic services, confer with government officials on the "spiritual aspects of democracy." He went everywhere, calling America's announced principles for the rebuilding of Japan "a bomb immeasurably greater than any ever dropped —the super-bomb of Christian love."

Summoned on several occasions to the Imperial Palace to "explain Christian democracy" to the Emperor, he said on one occasion, "Democracy, your majesty, is co-operation. Is it not significant that even our Japanese character for the word 'co-operation' has a Christian cross at its center?"

An impressive example of his contribution to the snobless social order decreed under Japan's new constitution occurred in the spring of 1947. Its beneficiary was the Eta (meaning "unclean") class, Japan's equivalent of India's "untouchables." As butchers and tanners, Buddhist aversion to animal killing had for centuries forced them into segregated villages. Now declared by law equal to any, elements among the Eta in villages surrounding Omi became outlaws, raiding mainline trains, robbing passengers, spreading terror, defying police.

Frantic railway officials finally appealed to Vories. He told them, "We'll tackle the problem if you and the police promise to keep your hands off. Give me a list of the leaders."

For the leaders of the eight gangs Merrell and Maki planned tea parties for eight successive Sunday afternoons, sending out formal invitations. On the first Sunday morning a young tough appeared. "Our leader can't come," he muttered. Invited in, he warily looked about for police. When by the second round of teas and cakes his belligerence had melted, Vories said amicably, "I asked you and your friends here because I need your help. I'm told there is much corruption among the police. I thought you could help us get the facts."

After hours during which the bandit vented his spleen against society, then stayed for lunch, a commotion suddenly arose outside. The entire gang was at the gate, shouting and brandishing sticks, obviously come to deliver their "captured" emissary. Merrell and Maki, the subdued ruffian between them, went to the gate, bowed them in. They swaggered inside, listened suspiciously to Vories' project. He said, "Everybody says you men are brave and strong, fearing nobody, not even the police." Then he added, "If you help me with this, I promise to do all I can to remove the disgraceful discrimination you and your people have suffered so long. Think it over. Meanwhile, our house is open to you. Bring your friends, any time."

During the next seven weeks, members of the gangs filtered in and out, savoring the arm-in-arm Vories friendliness, awed by their gracious acceptance by a lady of the nobility.

Nothing was said about railroad banditry until, finally, one gang leader volunteered, "Guess you've heard about those train robberies. We might help. But people won't trust us; they'll think we're gangsters." Vories replied, "I can fix that."

To railroad officials the next day he said casually, "I'm appointing some special police to ride the roads. I need passes and official armbands for these men." The officials glanced at his list and gasped, "But these are the very gangsters who've been terrorizing our trains!" Vories nodded. "Exactly," he said.

A few days later he distributed passes, armbands and assignments, then waited to see what would happen. Almost overnight all violence ceased. When it was plain that there would be no reoccurrence, the astounded railway heads asked, "How can we reward these men?" Vories replied, "As you would any other good citizens. Give them citations of appreciation—publicly."

The meeting, aglitter with formality and eloquent speeches by prefectural officials, followed by bowing and handshaking between police and former bandits, was the season's big event. All over the prefecture, the story of "When the bandits came to tea" became legend.

Having dramatized Eta fitness for integration into polite society, Vories moved to keep his promise. When leaders of a village with a segregated community asked him to lecture on "Democracy and Christianity" he accepted—on condition that the meeting be held in the Eta section. The former bandits spread word that "outsiders" were coming, promoted a mammoth clean-up campaign. Every street and gutter was scrubbed clean, every house made pin-neat. Visitors, astonished, returned to their communities after the meeting to say that they had misjudged the Eta, that ostracism for such people made no sense.

A few months later a "culture society" for youth, formed by the ex-gangsters, was invited to amalgamate with a similar group of the adjoining village. A big formal ceremony, held in the school auditorium, celebrated the event. Laudatory telegrams poured in from members of the central government in Tokyo. Newspapers throughout the country reported it as "a historic day for Japan's long-neglected minority group."

With equal facility Vories blunted the busy sickles of Communism when, after the war, Red activity broke out in Japan's universities. One night in 1947 the leader of a vigorous cell at Kyoto's Imperial University came to his door, tartly saying, "I'm an atheist and a Communist; you probably won't let me in." Vories replied with disarming friendliness, "Why not? I take it we're both interested in the same things: helping people to a better life."

After patient listening for hours to the Communist's glittering version of Red aims, Vories said, "It all sounds good. Perhaps you have some place where your principles have been practically applied—a sort of showcase I could look at?" When his visitor stammered, "Well, no—not yet," he said: "But we have. Come and see."

The young Red toured the Brotherhood's industrial depart-

ments, studied its social and economic platform, questioned
the workers, went away impressed. A few days later he
returned with the cell's full executive committee. Shortly
all nine were converted, turned their group into a Christian
cell instead! After graduation, the young leader went into the
tanning industry, today operates a large plant whose principles are modeled carefully after the Brotherhood's.

I could find nobody in Japan who ever heard Vories question the impulse that, a half century ago, dispatched him
across the seas into this place. He began without a dollar to
his name. "I still have no personal bank account," he told
me, "nor any expectation of ever having, nor any regret at
not having."

His serenity over his "bank-accountless" state was a puz-
zler to some. One day, dining with a friend of substance at
a swank New York club, he was told, "Merrell, you're the
biggest fool I ever met! You could have been a millionaire
—and you don't even own the house you live in!" Vories'
blue eyes twinkled, his thin face creasing in a smile, as he
pulled out some pictures of his Brotherhood, spread them on
the table, said quietly, "Who says I'm not wealthy?"

My visit to Omi coincided with the Brotherhood's annual
memorial service. Timed each year for the period when
cherry blossoms are in fullest bloom, the impressive ceremony
was established years ago in answer to Buddhist taunts that
"Christians do not honor their dead." Its site is a park-like
spot called "The Place of Perpetual Peace," at the base of a
hill topped by a lovely marble mausoleum.

We stood together beneath a pure white canopy stamped
with the Omi symbol and garlanded with flowers, watched
the assembly robed in their colorful kimonos, listened as they

sang hymns redolent of the Resurrection hope. The singing could be heard for miles around.

Then, at the service's climax, when those carrying the napkin-wrapped urns containing ashes of their dead started up the winding stone steps, climbing through lacy rows of cherry blossoms toward the mausoleum high above, Vories said softly:

"When the time comes for what's left of my mortal body to make that trip, I'd like for the Brotherhood to be singing, as they're singing now, 'O happy day that fixed my choice' . . ."

VI

Two Thousand Tongues to Go

When the boa constrictor struck, Loretta Anderson, a slight young woman from Paterson, New Jersey, was sitting alone in her dugout canoe beside an Indian settlement on the Morona River, deep in the Peruvian jungle. Her partner—Lila Wistrand, a nurse from Houston, Texas—had just climbed the river bank to treat a sick child. Suddenly the giant reptile surged out of the water and lashed at Loretta. Screaming, fighting off the monster, Loretta managed to leap from the canoe, dripping blood from a badly gashed hand and arm. Lila came on the run, dressed her wounds—and an hour later both were back at work patiently teaching the Shapra Indians to read and write.

At about the same time, some 800 miles to the southeast, Esther Matteson of Oakland, California, and Annie Shaw of Alberta, Canada, fever-ridden themselves, were battling an influenza epidemic that threatened to wipe out the Piro Indians along the turbulent Urubamba River. A couple of hundred miles northeast of them, Mary Ruth Wise of De-Witt, Arkansas, and Martha Duff of Lenoir City, Tennessee, aboard a balsa raft loaded with Amuesha Indians, were fighting rapids and treacherous whirlpools on their way to the jungle school they had set up on the banks of the Chuchurras River below the Peruvian Andes. And a bird's-eye view of the rest of Peru's 230,000 square miles of primeval wilderness would have revealed scores of other tiny jungle stations where other young Americans—42 of them unmarried girls of college age—were stopping tribal wars, fighting superstition and witchcraft, living dangerously among wild Indians. All for one purpose: to coax aborigines, whose languages have never before been reduced to writing, to learn the mysteries of "the paper that talks," the printed word.

These young Americans, and some 700 others like them, belong to one of the most determined and effective groups now waging war on world illiteracy: the Summer Institute of Linguistics (SIL), otherwise known as the Wycliffe Bible Translators. Currently at work among 175 different language groups in 12 countries, SIL linguists have a transfiguring glory in their vision. Braving almost unbelievable hazards, they quietly spend their lives analyzing unwritten Indian languages, creating primers and dictionaries, setting up schools and training native teachers.

The man who gives this group their vision is William Cameron Townsend—"Uncle Cam" to his associates—who has spent more than 40 years among Latin America's Indian tribes. I learned about Townsend one day in late 1957 while hitching a ride across the Andes in a Peruvian military-transport plane. As we swept past a 21,000 foot snow-capped peak and began a long glide down toward the jungle, the young pilot removed the oxygen tube from his teeth and gestured toward the vast wilderness stretching out ahead farther than the eye could see. "Many young *Norteamericanos* are out there," he beamed. "You know *Señor* Townsend and his *Instituto Linguistico?*"

When I looked blank, his face expressed pity. "You should go and see," he said. "Peruvians are proud of what the *Instituto* does for our country."

During the next few days, penetrating deep into the jungle by tiny missionary plane and tipsy dugout canoe, I did go and see. In Indian villages dotted along the twisting jungle rivers I watched these amazing young Americans conquering by Christian love, savage peoples whom neither time nor ancient Incas nor Spanish conquistadors had ever been able to conquer. And in their midst, spurring them on, was the remarkable man with the eager heart and the quick, boyish smile, whose dream had catapulted them into this audacious onslaught against ignorance and superstition.

Cam Townsend early developed his urge for spreading the Christian gospel. Back in 1917, when he was 21, he quit Occidental College in Los Angeles, packed a trunk with Spanish-language Bibles and headed for Guatemala. He soon found his Bibles a drug on the market. More than two thirds of Guatemala's population were Indians: few knew Spanish, fewer still showed any hankering to learn.

One day an Indian to whom Cam had offered a copy of the Bible demanded, "Why, if your God is so smart, hasn't He learned our language?" Then and there, Townsend quit Bible distribution in favor of giving God another tongue.

For the next 15 years he lived with the primitive Cakchiquel tribe in Guatemala, eating their food (one diet item: toasted ants), mastering their difficult tongue, gradually reducing it to written form. Slowly and laboriously, he developed a simplified method for teaching *any* phonetically written language.

When finally in 1932, racked with tuberculosis, Townsend

rode out again to civilization on a mule, he left the Cakchiquel Indians with five schools, a small hospital, a printing
plant, scores of small churches and hundreds of literate converts to Christianity. In Cam Townsend's soul was exulta-
tion; in his saddlebags was a printed copy, in the hitherto
unwritten Cakchiquel language, of the entire New Testament.

Back in the States, while recovering from the TB, he was
visited by an old missionary friend, Leonard Legters, who
urged him to do for other Latin-American Indians what he
had done for the Cakchiquels.

Townsend thought it over, finally said, "Okay, Leonard,
I'll tackle it. But on one condition: that you'll help me found
a pioneer training camp where we can train mission candidates in primitive-language reduction and Bible translating.
We're going to need a lot of help to do the job I have in
mind."

As a starter, the two men waded into statistical tomes on
illiteracy, and were astounded to find that almost half the
world's adult population could neither read nor write. Even
more astounding was the fact that there were in the world
some 3000 separate and distinct languages, more than 2000
of them without any translations from the Bible at all.

"That's our goal," declared Cam. "Two thousand tongues
to go!"

In the summer of 1934, Townsend and Legters opened
their school in an abandoned farmhouse in the Arkansas
Ozarks. For the first session only two students showed up,
but by its eighth summer the school had outgrown the farmhouse—and a renovated chicken-coop used for sleeping quar-

ters—and moved to the campus of the University of Oklahoma.

Incorporated as the Summer Institute of Linguistics, this unique school now teaches language analysis to some 500 students annually at the Universities of Oklahoma, North Dakota and Washington, has branches in England, Canada and Australia. Graduates to date number more than 4000, are at work in 25 countries under mission boards of 35 denominations, both Protestant and Catholic.

Students taking the required SIL courses for two summers of 11 weeks each concentrate on no specific tongue. Instead, they are drilled intensively in the general principles basic to all language analysis. Once a student has learned to recognize and reproduce phonetically the hundreds of known speech sounds, he is taught how to create a workable alphabet, develop a dictionary, work up a "grammar," construct primers and teach illiterates to read.

But before being whooshed into SIL's wilderness orbit, the student linguists are put through the wringer during three months of rugged "survival tests" at a jungle training camp. Here both men and women must prove themselves able to handcraft their own jungle huts without saw, hammer or nails (they use wild-cane poles, and leaves); make balsa rafts and handle dugout canoes through raging rapids and crocodile-infested rivers; cope with wild animals and giant reptiles; administer first aid for everything from broken bones to epidemics; and find their way on 25-mile hikes through unmarked forests, living off the jungle. Those who pass these rigorous tests—more than 90 per cent—are then sent out for three months of living with "test tribes." Here they prove further their ability to "take it."

As soon as he had trained a few in his linguistic method, Townsend and his students headed for Mexico. They were stopped at the border, bluntly told, "We don't want translators. The Indian languages must disappear." Townsend retorted, "They disappear more rapidly if you use the Indians' languages to teach them Spanish."

With help from two noted Mexicans, educator Moisés Sáenz and Dr. Mariano Silva y Aceves, a linguist, he wormed his way in, settled among the Aztecs in the state of Morelos, started on the long job of making friends and learning the language.

Cam Townsend and his wife were living in a rickety cartrailer in the shabby village of Tetelcingo when, one day, President Lazaro Cardenas came through on a tour of his nation's hinterland. Seeing the sandy-haired, soft-spoken young American sitting in front of his trailer surrounded by Indians, Cardenas halted his car in a cloud of dust and strolled over.

Amazed, Cardenas listened to the American's explanation as to what he was doing here, then blurted, "I wish we had a hundred like you." Townsend replied, "I'll see that you get them, Your Excellency."

Today, with the full co-operation of the government, there are in Mexico 216 SIL translators, working among 51 backward tribes. "We don't look upon you as foreigners any more," a high government official said recently. "You're real Mexicans!"

Typical of Townsend's dedicated workers is Marianna Slocum of Ardmore, Pa. Marianna and her fiancé studied at SIL, preparing to go together to the Tzeltals, a tribe numbering some 40,000 in the state of Chiapas. When her fiancé died just before the wedding date, Marianna insisted on following their gleam alone.

"My family was horrified," she says. "But they came around."

After mastering the complicated language, Marianna prepared school texts, started reading and writing classes and —in 16 years—founded seven thriving bilingual schools, translated into Tzeltal a raft of books and pamphlets introducing the tribesmen to the Mexican national culture. Along the way, she managed to banish witchcraft, thievery and drunkenness from large sections of the tribe, replace witch-doctors' nostrums with modern medicine and convert 5000 Tzeltals from sun worship to Christianity.

Last December, as Marianna packed up to move on to another dialect, a leading Mexican magazine, *Tiempo*, made her the subject of a 16-column cover story that proclaimed her "the architect of a transformed situation." She had lifted an entire Indian nation "from barbarism to civilization."

Meanwhile, word of SIL's achievements in Mexico was spreading to other Latin-American countries. Joyously, Cam Townsend helped spread it. Invited to conferences of Pan-American educators, he found ready agreement among them that any nation that ignored its large aboriginal population was committing a criminal waste of human and national resources. To those who gloomily opined that it was impossible to find enough dedicated linguists among their own people, he said, "We're training hundreds of young Americans who ask for nothing but a chance to help you with the job."

Peru was first to respond to Cam Townsend's offer of trained linguists. In the summer of 1945, at the invitation of

President Manuel Prado, he spent months surveying the Peruvian jungle, visiting tribal headmen, sounding out their willingness. Then he brought in workers for three of the most remote tribes. To get to them, the young North Americans had to travel for weeks by canoe and raft, beat their way through almost impenetrable jungle, detour around tribes noted for killing white men on sight.

This harrowing experience convinced Townsend of one thing: "We've got to have a plane." A U.S. Marine mission at Lima was about to scrap an old Grumman amphibian. The Peruvian government, with a generous assist from a Townsend admirer in California, bought it for him, and to fly it Townsend recruited Larry Montgomery, a former Air Force combat flier. Today Montgomery is superintendent of JAARS (Jungle Aviation and Radio Service), SIL's air arm.

JAARS now has a fleet of 19 planes, 21 pilots, plus crews of maintenance men and skilled radio technicians. Most of the aircraft are equipped with pontoons for river landings. Workhorse of the fleet is a Navy-surplus PBY, used for hauling heavy loads to jungle outposts and for transporting 50-gallon drums of emergency gasoline which are cached at convenient places along the rivers. The Catalina bears the name "Moisés Sáenz," in whose memory a group of Mexicans donated its purchase money. Pride of the fleet is the Helio Courier, a lately developed stallproof, spinproof all-metal plane that can take off or land in 75 yards at only 30 m.p.h. when fully loaded, cruise at 160 m.p.h. and as high as 23,000 feet, turn in a small radius at low speeds and, using an ingenious winch, can hoist a man out of the jungle while flying a tight circle close to the ground.

Last year Townsend's daring pilots flew more than a million and a half air miles over the "green hell" of Peru's Amazonia without a single injury to any passenger or crewman. I saw for myself the hazards of such flying. One JAARS flier told me, "Hang on. We have to do tricks with these small planes that were never dreamed of by their manufacturers—except in nightmares." Pilots must find their way over country where all existing maps are inaccurate. Daily they put their planes down safely on postage-stamp landing strips gashed out of the jungle or make tricky river landings on crocodile-infested waters.

All dangers are not in landings. On one occasion, when JAARS Pilot Leo Lance stepped off his pontoon into knee-deep water to secure his plane to a tree, a cry from a naked Indian on the bank startled him. Following the Indian's quivering finger, Leo saw swimming toward him a vicious *fer de lance*. While desperately hanging onto the rope of his fast-drifting plane, he had to fight off with a stick the water viper whose bite brings death in a matter of minutes.

Flying alone on most of their missions, pilots not infrequently have to come down for minor repairs, must be able to make their own. If dusk overtakes them, they must put down for the night in jungle opening or on the river.

Whimsicalities of jungle weather and rainfall often present problems. One night, after securing his plane to a tree, Larry Montgomery left an Indian on guard while he walked to the nearest Indian village two hours away through dense jungle. In the middle of the night, the Indian guard ran in breathlessly to report, "Big bird drowning!" Racing back to the river, Larry found it had risen 10 feet; his plane, almost submerged, was held by the ropes from rising with it. Loosening the ropes, he climbed aboard to spend the rest of the night. In the morning, as the water went down, he had to slit holes in the fabric to let the water out, then patch them up with random strips of cloth. After drying out the water-logged engine, then washing off the heavy weight of silt and mud caking the wings, he took off on his rounds, "a little lopsided but finally airborne."

In flight each pilot packs an air mattress, mosquito net, machete and survival rations, keeps in constant touch with SIL's radio tower at its jungle base, relays weather information from tribal workers, stands ready at a moment's notice to go to the aid of a linguist or a fellow-pilot in trouble.

As Omer Bondurant, 35-year-old veteran of a World War II night-fighter squadron, told me, "We do our best, then leave the rest to God."

When Townsend is not gadding about the world scouting out hitherto unreached Indian tribes, recruiting college youths, selling governments on his literacy program, he is "at home" at Yarinacocha, the staging area for SIL's Operation Peru. A 400-acre slash in the jungle, this base is a humming beehive of activity devoted to one end: the servicing and supplying of the young linguists who are currently at work among 29 of Peru's 45 different tribal groups, each with its own distinct language, customs—and jeopardies.

Catch him at home and Townsend will take you through the big base sprawled out along the shores of Lake Yarina. Here are the hangars, repair shops and airstrips for his air force. Here, too, are the jungle-style residences for 175 workers and their families; a medical clinic; commissary; cafeteria and dormitories for tribal workers constantly passing in and out; a printing shop where tribal primers, dictionaries and other reading materials are manufactured—some 18,000 volumes in 1957. Here, also, are classrooms where Indians brought in from their tribes may be given advanced training under Ministry of Education supervision, taught Spanish, then returned as teachers of their own people in newly established government schools.

Nerve center of the jungle base is Radio Central, a control tower manned day and night to keep contact with linguists out among the tribes. "A translator," Townsend told me, "may be deposited by plane in a howling wilderness, but unless he has a radio transmitter for communication with headquarters, the chances of his remaining long enough to get his job done are slim." Thus, shortly after beginning the jungle work, he bought, scrounged or had given him enough war-surplus radio sets to bind his whole far-reaching jungle program into a radio network.

Dramatic incidents proving the network's value occur with alarming frequency. There was, for example, the time when an SIL team used its transmitter to quash a tribal war in the making. While among the Cashinahuas (known as the "Bat People"), Eugene Scott and Kenneth Kensinger found their tribe seething one day with war preparations. The Cashinahuas had just heard a rumor that one of their men, who had married into the neighboring Culina tribe, had been the victim of a witchcraft slaying by his in-laws. Brandishing spears and bows and arrows, they shouted, "Death to all Culinas!"

"How do you know the rumor is true?" Scott asked the Indians. "Come, let's check."

Mystified, the warriors crowded around the transmitter while a call was put through to an SIL team living with the Culinas. In a matter of minutes the voice of the "murdered" man, 100 miles distant, was reassuring his kinsmen: he was not only alive but was being treated well by "our friends the Culinas." The warriors dropped their weapons. Their chief asked to speak to his Culina opposite number, invited the Culinas to a big feast. Three days later what might have been a bloody battle was turned into an intertribal whoopla for peace.

Linguists in the jungles are required to make radio contact regularly; if they are "off the air" too long, a plane is dispatched to discover why. A staff of radio technicians circulates regularly among the stations to see that transmitters and receivers are in top condition.

One girl, working with one of the Jivaro head-shrinking tribes, told me of the time when, having gone three hours downriver to reach scattered members of her tribe, she became so absorbed that she "just plain forgot to report in." Paddling back upstream, a trip requiring 15 hours, she arrived at her shack on the river "just in time to welcome a plane zooming in from a five-hour flight to rescue me. They've never let me forget that!"

On occasion the radio tower at Yarinacocha knits SIL's whole sprawling operation into a network of prayer. The operator on duty may alert the entire network as follows: "For the next hour Pilot George Insley will be over jungle area where he cannot land. . . . Wes and Eva Thiesen report their Indians threatened with flash floods. . . . Uncle Cam leaving today to address college groups in States, seeking new workers. . . . Pilot Don Smith forced down on river, engine trouble. All request your prayers. That is all."

The girl linguists go out into these incredibly dangerous places as casually and eagerly as their sisters at home explore a shopping center. And they seem to make out better than the men—probably because the Indians are less suspicious of them. As Dr. Townsend says, "The Indian chiefs think, 'They're only women. What harm can they do? Like as not they're looking for husbands.' "

Townsend was at first skittish about sending girls into unpredictable tribal situations alone. But he was shamed into it when, several years ago, two volunteers demanded, "You say that God takes care of His own. Doesn't that include us?"

He let them go. "And of course God honored their faith," he says. "He has taken perfect care of them."

In all Peru I found no better example of this care—or of the amazing courage of SIL's girl linguists—than Loretta Anderson, pioneer among the Shapra tribe.

Eight years ago the Shapras, vicious killers and head-hunters, were among the most feared of Peruvian tribes. Their chief, a regal but bloodthirsty savage named Tariri, had attained leadership by the simple device of slaying his predecessor in cold blood, then daring any wariror to dispute his authority. Then one day in 1950 Loretta, with her first co-worker, Doris Cox, paddled up to his village in a dugout canoe. Climbing the river bank, between rows of glowering tribesmen momentarily immobilized by such audacity, the two slender white girls faced the chief. Using a few Shapra words picked up from a trader downriver, plus sign language, they told him they had come to live among his people and study their language.

One of the Shapra words they inadvertently dropped in the one-sided conversation was "brother." Only later they learned how fortuitous was its use, that by it they had bound

Tariri to protect them—since by tribal law Shapra men must defend their sisters.

Tariri stared at the two girls in a long silence. Then he crisply ordered that they be assigned a hut, with a couple of older Indian women to help them with whatever they were after. Years later he confided to Townsend, "If you had sent men, we would have killed them on sight. Or if a couple, I'd have killed the man and taken the woman for myself. But what could a great chief do with two harmless girls who insisted on calling him brother?"

The jungle surrounding their hut had its beauty: clouds of lavishly colored butterflies fluttering through shafts of brilliant sunshine that pierced the foliage when the rains stopped; gaudy toucans, macaws and umbrella birds swooping through the trees. It also had its sinister sounds. At night, from the dripping forest, came the cries of howler monkeys and the jaguar's coughing roar.

Most discomforting were the hordes of flying and crawling things: gnats that swarmed about them by day; the ants and cockroaches that came out of every crevice of their hut, the big spiders that crawled over their bed nets at night.

For months Tariri, busy with his wars, left the girls to their mysterious devices—though they learned from others in the tribe that he got regular reports on their doings. Often the whole tribe, men and women, would leave the village for days at a time, for feasts, hunts, fiestas. Alone in the village, the girls often wondered whether they were being abandoned. Today they scoff when you call them courageous.

"We were scared most of the time during the first five months," Doris and Loretta will tell you. "But when we trembled the most we prayed the hardest."

They prayed hard one night when, while they were working over their notes by candlelight, an Indian woman burst
in with alarming news. The men of the tribe, winding up a
drunken feast, were even now reeling down the path to the
hut, loudly proclaiming their intention to attack the white
girls. "You must hide!"

The girls fled to the forest, spent the night there. Next
morning, returning to their radio transmitter, they called
Yarinacocha, 400 miles away.

"Bring Tariri to the radio," said the base director, Harry
Goodall.

The chief, who understood Spanish, heard a stern voice
coming from the black box. It said, "You are the chief—and
you can't control your tribe?"

His authority challenged, Tariri drew himself up with
solemn dignity. "I am the chief," he said. "I promise that the
señoritas will not be harmed."

And they weren't, then or later.

Amid such harassments, Loretta and Doris buckled down
to the agonizingly slow job of learning the language, desperately trying to distinguish one sound from another in the
exotic jargon that swirled about them. After several months
the white girls' persistence, plus their many kindly acts,
melted the Shapras' suspicions. Flattered by the girls' earnest
attempts to master their language, the Indians readily gave
them words for objects pointed at, and the language note-
books began to fill up with Shapra words and phrases. As
soon as they had a phonetic alphabet worked out, Doris and
Loretta began the long task of producing primers, teaching
Shapra children to read and write. Along with Shapra folk

stories and legends, they translated a few verses from the Bible.

Abruptly one day Chief Tariri joined a little group the girls were teaching. He stood, frowning, as the lesson went on. After hearing the first Scripture verse translated into his own language, he broke in to ask that it be repeated again and again. Finally he exclaimed, "My heart understands with a leap!"

To Doris and Loretta he said, "When you came, I did not understand why. Now I know. What you are doing makes my people happier and better able to care for themselves."

Thereafter the chief appeared regularly at the girls' hut, would sit for hours helping them get the exact meanings of words, write down tribal stories, translate more Bible verses. And as he did so, Tariri began to show signs of subtle change. One day in 1953, three years after the girls had come to his village, he called his Shapras together for a dramatic announcement.

"I like this white girls' God," he said. "He has brought us many good things. I'm going to stop worshiping the boa."

He became more and more insistent on Bible translation. Hovering over them as they struggled to get more verses down, he impatiently demanded one day, "How can we remember God's word and live as He wants us to live when it isn't written down on paper for us to see?"

In the following months, Doris and Loretta were convinced that Tariri was indeed changed. Not only did he put aside snake worship, but, one by one, without being asked to, he shrugged off witch-doctor practices, outlawed murder, abolished head-shrinking.

In 1955, when Townsend arranged a celebration of SIL's

tenth anniversary in Peru, he took Tariri with him to Lima. With Loretta translating for him, Tariri talked unabashedly with Peru's president, newspaper editors, groups of school children. Every inch a chief, even in the white man's jungle, he held his head high, told Loretta, "Speak up, leave out nothing I say."

Two years later, in June 1957, Townsend arranged for Tariri and Loretta to go to Hollywood to appear on Ralph Edwards' "This Is Your Life" TV show. The program featured Rachel Saint, an SIL translator who had helped Loretta briefly with the Shapras but who is now writing the language of the Aucas, savage slayers of her brother, Nate Saint, and four other young missionaries. Tariri caught the fancy of viewers: millions will remember how he stood proudly self-possessed, stared boldly into the camera's eye and testified with simple dignity to his new-found faith.

The quality of Tariri's commitment to Christian precepts underwent a fiery test when, returning to his jungle fastness, he was attacked by an enemy group. He was shot through the chest, and others of his Shapras were slain. Jungle law called for bloody reprisal, but Tariri's faith was strong. He issued an order for his revenge-hungry Shapras to simmer down, called the girls to him and said, "Read, please, where God says, 'Return not evil for evil.'"

Tariri got a test of a different sort later—and passed it equally well. A well-meaning merchant in Lima, during one of the chief's forays into civilization, showed Tariri the wonders of an outboard motor, promised to send him one for his dugout canoe. Unfortunately, the merchant left the details of filling the order to a clerk who thought "anything is good enough for an Indian." Thus when, a few weeks later, the chief unpacked the wooden box, his face fell. Instead of the shiny new one he had seen, the motor was a battered model that wouldn't work.

This first brush with civilized duplicity left Tariri's faith intact but his hackles high. With Loretta taking down his exact words, he dictated a scorching letter of remonstrance to his "benefactor." In it his newly acquired religious faith struggled with his inbred impulse to retaliate for such an offense against chiefly dignity.

"Señor," he wrote, "I was happy when you said you would send me a motor. I told my children. I told all the men in my village. I thought you were good. I did not ask you to help me. It was your own idea. You looked into my eyes. I prayed God to help you because you were sending me a motor. Then this bad motor came. I'm sad. God's heart is sad too. Don't do that again. If you want to help someone, really help him. Among ourselves we don't send bad things to a chief."

While keeping himself in Christian check, Tariri could not refrain from recalling what might have happened under other circumstances and previous customs. He said: "We used to raid and take the women and kill the young men, then take their heads. When people sent bad messages to us, we said, 'Because they want to die, they do that!' Then we'd go and kill them."

Then he concluded: "That's the way we used to do, before the girls came. Now we have left that. I'm not talking with anger. I'm talking softly. It is because you don't know Jesus that you do things like that. But I love you even though you did that. I pray for you. But what you did to me, don't do again!" The embarrassed donor sent new parts for the motor. And today the chief goes up and down the river four times as fast as he used to.

By such trials Tariri's faith has battled its way to triumph over inbred tribal bloodthirst and modern loose-dealing.

Today there are a number of Shapra schools going, with primers and other teaching tools in the Shapra language. Young tribesmen now in training will shortly become qualified teachers. Nearly 100 Shapras have followed Tariri in accepting Christianity. The Gospel of Mark, in the Shapra tongue, is completed and ready for printing. And in tribal celebrations along the Morona River, Christian hymns are now sung in place of the former sonnets to blood lust and head-shrinking.

Still, the work is far from done. Another five to seven years must be spent with the Shapras before the girls can move on to another tribe and another long battle with a new tongue.

"It's not easy," says Loretta Anderson. "But it's a lot of fun. And how rewarding!"

I discovered this same attitude among every SIL linguist group I met. Hardest pressed are those who work with tribes whose languages are multi-tonal. For example, take the Ticunas, who live far down the Amazon, and whose tongue has five distinct tones. Each word in Ticuna may mean five radically different things, according to the tone used.

Notifying one such tribe that they were leaving briefly for a conference with Townsend, two girl linguists announced that "The boss has sent for us"—only to learn by the tribe's horrified reaction that they'd actually said, "The *devil* has

sent for us!" And the superstitious people believed them—at
first. In another such tribe, the words for "sinner" and "fat
person" are the same: the tone used spells the difference. One
day, teaching that "God loves the sinner," the worker saw be-
wilderment on his Indians' faces. To his dismay he discovered
he'd been asserting that "God loves the fat person." Since
few in the tribe were fat, he was "shutting out a lot of them
from divine favor." He quickly shifted to the right tone.

But the SIL people have to sandwich their linguistic work
in between treating countless ills. For, in dispatching a pair
of workers into the jungle, Townsend likes to have one of
them a trained nurse, and both must be prepared to cope
with the health emergencies which arise in dismaying abun-
dance. Pneumonia is rife—and deadly. Common, too, are ele-
phantiasis, yaws and an ulcerating disease called *leishmania-
sis* which, transmitted by a sand fly, destroys nose and throat
passages and brings death from starvation.

I found a good example of the linguist-nurse in Jeannie
Grover, a serene, blue-eyed girl from Pateros, Washington
Jeannie's tribe is the Aguarunas, a branch of the head-hunting Jivaros, largest Indian grouping (10,000) in Peru's Amazon basin. Among them Jeannie and her partner, Millie
Larson from Solway, Minnesota, have established 11 bilingual schools. In one-room, thatch-roofed schoolhouses scattered over the jungle-covered hills, some 600 little boys and
girls are taught by Aguaruna men who, a few years ago, could
not read or write their own language but who are now proficient in both it and Spanish. In June 1956 the 11 teachers
from these schools went to the polls to vote in the Peruvian
elections—for the first time in Aguaruna history.

Jeannie's and Millie's hut is in a tiny patch of clearing, edged on one side by the tumbling Marañon River, on three others by dense jungle. When not off fighting their enemies, Aguaruna men mill about the clearing, fondling their blow-guns and poison-tipped darts, laughing and talking. I commented that the Aguarunas, with their reputation as murderous head-shrinkers, looked pretty formidable—these barrel-chested bronze men in short skirts, erect and proud of visage, their upper bodies daubed with red paint and decorated with beetle wings and toucan feathers. Jeannie laughed merrily. "They looked so to me, at first. Now they're the most beautiful people on earth!"

Every day some 30 Indians come to her hut for first aid or medical treatment. To reach other patients she must tramp through the dripping forests, a banana leaf over her head for an umbrella, her medical kit in hand, or travel by dugout canoe up the turbulent river.

Does she feel no fear? "Only one—that some day, when we need it most, we'll run out of medicine!"

That fear was justified when, not long ago, Jeannie's Aguarunas came down with 200 cases of dysentery, exhausting her stock of remedies. But a radio message to Yarinacocha brought swift answer. The doctor there loaded a plane with medicines, flew to Jeannie's aid and, after ten days of furious labors up and down the Marañon, had the epidemic stopped in its tracks.

"Before Millie and I came," Jeannie told me, "the witch doctor was in sole charge of the Aguarunas' health. When confronting a patient, he first fortifies himself with a long drink of potent *ayahuasca.* Then, alternating drinks with puffs on his pipe, he sucks on the surface of the sick area—often until the blood comes—and spits on the ground. Next he does a wild dance around the victim, cursing at the spot where he spat. When the *ayahuasca* takes hold, he falls to the ground. Anyone whose face shows up in his drunken dream is declared to be the black-magic worker who caused the sickness, and the alleged culprit is promptly banished, or killed if the patient dies."

"Nowadays," says Jeannie, "I'm afraid we are doing him out of a job." The witch-doctor still goes through his shenanigans, but with less authority and fewer patients. In fact, not long ago when his own daughter fell ill, he brought her in his arms to beg for a hypo injection and sulfa salve for the sores covering the little body. "White man's sickness," he grunted—and turned his daughter over to Jeannie.

Jeannie regards her tribe with affection, their less murderous peccadillos with amusement. Do she and Millie, I asked, ever get lonely in this far pocket of primeval man? Her blue eyes twinkled as she said wryly, "A lonely moment is what we crave most!"

The base clinic at Yarinacocha, started in 1949 by Dr. Kenneth Altig with a second-hand doctor's kit and a batch of donated medicines, now boasts a 12-room building, up-to-date laboratory equipment including X-ray, and serves 10,000 patients annually. Its medical stores are supplied partly by the Peruvian public health service, partly by friendly pharmaceutical houses in the States.

In charge of the always-crowded clinic is Dr. Ralph Eichenberger, the busiest and most resourceful medical director I have ever met. With only a skeleton nursing staff ("I have trouble keeping nurses—they all want to go out into the tribes!") he manages a round-the-clock program of healing that must surely be unique. Besides doctoring patients flown in from the jungles, he keeps in touch with the linguist-nurses by radio, and stands ready at a moment's notice to take off into the wilderness to meet emergencies.

Dr. Eichenberger likens his work to that of a city's public health service. "The only difference," he says, "is that our 'city' covers a quarter-million square miles, our 'visiting nurses' are hundreds of jungle miles apart, our 'consultation' is by radio, our 'ambulances' are balsa rafts and jungle-hopping planes." Covering this circuit, containing 130,000 disease-prone tribespeople, takes some doing.

Since 1954, when many lepers were found living along the Ucayali River, Drs. Eichenberger and Altig have conducted monthly "leper flights." On these rounds they stop at dozens of little villages, or meet in prearranged spots along the river those who have been banished from their tribes. The sufferers paddle out to the pontooned plane in canoes from their jungle hideouts, lift their disfigured faces and hands in mute appeal. During the last four years hundreds of Indians, their leprosy arrested, have been returned to their tribes.

SIL's linguist-nurses must necessarily perform medical services far beyond the portfolio of the average graduate nurse. But when they have a complicated case, they call Dr. Eichenberger. This tireless, devoted man at his radio, his calm voice reaching out across huge distances to prescribe treatment, provides a picture whose drama is lost only on himself.

For example, when his radio crackled out the news that a young Piro Indian girl had suffered a compound fracture of her elbow that resisted the usual setting, he called for an exact description of the break, told the nurse how to rig up rocks for weights to pull the shattered bones back into place and how to apply tree branches for splints. Ten days later, visiting the tribe on his regular rounds, he found that the break was healing perfectly.

Then there was the Indian bitten by the deadly bush-master and left by his tribesmen to die. The linguist, lacking antivenin, was told: "You have a kerosene refrigerator? Pack his foot in ice. I'm on the way." Within a few hours, Dr. Eichenberger had the man back at the clinic, an operation performed, and his life saved.

When a worker with the Huambisa tribe frantically called in to report a mother dying in complicated childbirth, Eich-enberger crisply ordered: "Take your radio into the woman's hut. Leave your receiver turned on. Do exactly what I tell you." With his instructions, the birth was successfully accom-plished. Both mother and baby lived. Hours later, the worker called back: "Hear that racket, Doc? The whole tribe's cele-brating. They say you're the greatest witch-doctor that ever lived!"

How do the SIL workers make these Amazonian Indians *want* to learn? Says Townsend, "We trade upon three facets in their mentality that are common to almost all primitives: their pride in their own language, their eagerness to better themselves economically, their insatiable curiosity."

It is Townsend's theory that "jungle Indians are the most curious people alive. Only the fear of other tribes, plus gen-erations of mistreatment by the only outsiders they've met —rubber workers, gold seekers, adventurers—has prevented them from learning about ideas, people, happenings in the mysterious world beyond their green-walled prison. The mind of the Amazonian primitive is an inexhaustible well of curiosity. Just provide a pump, prime it a little—then step back and watch it flow!"

Out in the jungle I saw his theory validated again and again. In one tribe I watched a linguist with a young beginner. She pointed to a symbol she had created for the word "tree," let the youngster observe it for several minutes. Then she flipped to a page with this symbol among dozens of others. "Now find the tree," she said. The boy's eager eyes searched the page. Then, suddenly, his brown finger stabbed at one symbol and his face lighted up as he said, "Teacher, *I'm reading!*"

"Once they discover reading is possible," she told me, "there's no stopping them."

The incentive to learn to write is likewise easy to stir in Indians. The idea of communicating with each other by "the paper that talks" intrigues them. Too, they quickly catch on to writing's value as a prod to memory. One tribe, watching their linguist at work, noticed how she would stumble and stutter while trying to recall the correct word —then, after a glance at her notebook, burst forth with it. They said, "We wish we had something to help us remember too!" Thereafter, when telling her something they wanted to be sure she'd remember, they always said, "Write it down, Teacher!"—confident that if the matter was committed to paper, she would not forget.

The advantage of learning a second language—Spanish, in the case of Peru—also quickly becomes apparent to jungle Indians. Especially to those who have dealings with itinerant traders and *patrones* who settle near their borders, establish trading posts, supply them with trinkets in exchange for Indian goods—and often exploit their ignorance by bilking them.

There was, for example, the Indian who proudly bounced into the hut of an SIL linguist, flourishing what looked like a 1000-*peso* banknote. "See how much money I got from a trader who wanted my lumber!" he beamed. The linguist glanced at the bogus bill, sadly shook her head. "It's worthless," she said. "Only used by children for playing store." The Indian's face fell, his anger rose. "He could do that to me because I'm illiterate," he fumed. "Please teach me!"

It was this kind of situation, Townsend told me, that impelled Chief Shironkama of the Machiguengas to seek education for his people. Throughout Peru's Amazonia, Shironkama is acknowledged as one of the most powerful and, until recently, one of the most feared of tribal headmen. Today he and many of his formerly savage warriors are striking examples of the changes that SIL workers can bring about in a few years of concentrated effort.

To get Shironkama's story firsthand, I took off one day from Yarinacocha for the far Urubamba River. Our pontoon-equipped Cessna, flown by JAARS Pilot Don Weber, soared for hours over thick jungle broken only by occasional twisting rivers. Suddenly, far below, we saw one of the villages of Shironkama's domain.

Coming down low over the river, Weber muttered, "It's in flood. Look at that clutter!" I glanced down—and was all for turning back. The river was a raging torrent, filled with logs. Weber calmly moved his stick and grinned. "Ever hear of coming in on a wing and a prayer?"

Second later we splashed to a landing and Weber maneuvered us toward the shore, skillfully dodging the drifting debris. As the pontoons nudged the muddy bank, he leaped from the cockpit and flung a rope to some excited Indians who quickly secured the plane to a tree.

Atop the bank stood a solitary figure, clothed from neck to ankle in a hand-woven *cushma*, the peculiar sack-like garment of the Machiguengas. This was Chief Shironkama, former "terror of the Urubamba." He gravely greeted us, was joined almost immediately by a handsome young man in a jungle helmet—Wayne Snell, SIL linguist from Elgin, Illinois. Standing together on that lonely bank, the two made a striking picture.

A gunner's mate during World War II, Wayne told me his call to missionary service had come when he met, on island after island in the South Pacific, black men who, instead of the raw savages he'd expected, "were better Christians than I was." They had been made so, he learned, by Christian missions. The war over, he took the SIL course, and volunteered for duty in Peru.

Since 1952, Wayne and his wife Betty have established a number of bilingual schools among the hitherto unreached Machiguengas; created textbooks on reading and writing, arithmetic, farming, health and hygiene; persuaded the prone-to-wander Indians to settle around the schools (initiating an agricultural program aimed at making it profitable to do so); and translated several portions of the Bible. To top it all, they have made a practicing Christian out of Shironkama.

Since his conversion three years ago, the chief's rigid rule for his large tribe has been: "No more killings; no more drunken feasts; no more raids on other tribes for women."

William C. Townsend (*left*), founder of the Summer Institute of Linguistics (Wycliffe Bible Translators), with Chief Tariri of the Shapras whose conversion to Christianity transformed an entire tribe of vicious Peruvian jungle head-hunters. (Chapter VI)

Yarinacocha, SIL's jungle base in Peru, seen from the air. Overhead are two of Townsend's "air force" of jungle-hopping planes which serve the far-flung tribes where linguists are at work.

SIL workers with jungle tribes must learn to handcraft their own jungle huts without benefit of hammer, saw or nails.

SIL linguists building a balsa raft for travel and transport of supplies to their remote jungle stations.

"Radio Central" at SIL's jungle base in Peru knits the widely scattered jungle workers into an efficient network of prayer and communication.

A young linguist-nurse with the Aguarunas, a branch of the head-hunting Jivaros, receiving medical advice via radio from the jungle base, hundreds of miles away.

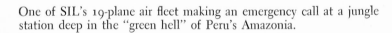

An SIL worker patiently waits her turn to prove that modern medicine, and not the witch-doctor's mumbo-jumbo, is the answer to severe sickness.

One of SIL's 19-plane air fleet making an emergency call at a jungle station deep in the "green hell" of Peru's Amazonia.

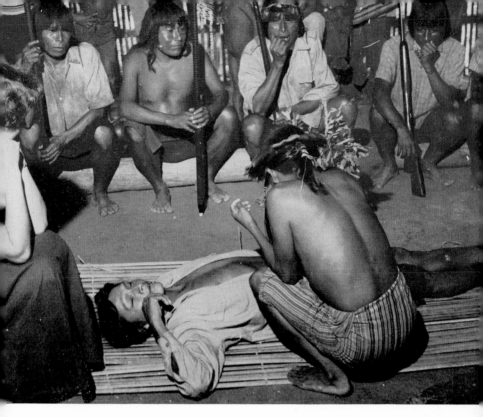

Once known as the "terror of the Urubamba," Chief Shironkama (shown here with SIL linguist Wayne Snell) is leading his Machiguengas toward Christian civilization.

To the little jungle schools come both Indian children and their parents, eager to learn to read the "paper that talks."

SIL linguist-nurses must be prepared to cope with a dismaying variety of physical ills and emergencies.

A young Indian, only a few years away from jungle savagery, who has been trained to be a teacher of his own people, at work in his outdoor school.

he author demonstrates the "flat eads" produced in e Peruvian tribe by nding with boards, re and aft, the eads of all babies.

For years, often as many as 15, a linguist must live with her adopted tribe, patiently learning the language and reducing it to written form.

Shironkama settled his own woman question by dismissing (with pensions) his plurality of wives, then asked Snell for legal marriage with the one he chose to keep.

The Snells' first contact with the chief was dramatic. They had scarcely settled in their native hut when their village, a day's canoe trip from Shironkama's, was raided. The chief, whose supply of wives was running low, had staged the raid to replenish his stock. When he and his warriors surged up to the Snells' hut, Shironkama stared in disbelief at the white couple, held his warriors back while listening to their reason for being there, then abruptly turned on his heel and left, cryptically grunting, "I'll be back."

One day shortly thereafter Shironkama reappeared, this time trailed by a group of children he had rounded up from several Machiguenga villages. To Snell he said, "You make school, yes?"

Only later did the Snells learn why Shironkama wanted education for his people. For years his Machiguengas had been victims of a white *patrón* who cheated them blind in trades, worked them for such pittance pay as one fishhook for a whole barrel of rice, indentured them with debt. When the Machiguengas, weary of such treatment, began staying away, the *patrón* called in Shironkama, told him he would have to force his people to work out their debts, gave the chief a gun, saying, "If they won't work, shoot them!" The chief took the gun, shot two of the *patrón's* henchmen instead. "The *patrón* will not make you his slaves again," he told his people. "You are free."

Chief Shironkama told me, with Snell interpreting: "From such white men as the *patrón* I learned that men who had power read books. I reasoned that, if one is to avoid being cheated or enslaved, he too must have the knowledge that books give. I wanted that knowledge for myself and my people."

The next morning before dawn I was bonged awake by someone beating on a hollow log. It was the bell announcing school's start an hour later. The Indians were already assembled outside the one-room schoolhouse; they'd been up, I found, since 3:30.

Chief Shironkama was herding the students, ranging from very small to near-manhood, into the building whose thatched roof was still dripping from the night's torrential rains. When they were all in, the rough benches behind rude desks filled, Shironkama himself sat on the floor, leaning against the bamboo-pole wall.

School began with a Bible reading. The lesson dealt with John the Baptist's manful defiance of Herod. As it was explained in fluent Machiguenga, I watched the chief's face. It was alight with understanding. With every point Snell made, Shironkama nodded thoughtfully, and from his throat came the murmuring assent, "Mmm-mmm-mmm."

Instruction was then taken over by a young Indian named Mario, whom the Snells had carefully developed into teacher and village Christian leader. While Mario's voice droned on, the chief's sharp eyes searched the faces of the students to see if they were listening. They were—intently.

These students, Mario told me later, wanted to have classes all day. They scorned recesses, barely taking time out to eat. At dismissal of school they gathered in small groups to compete in display of their new knowledge. I noticed one youngster, about 14, saunter off to the river bank, a primer under his arm. He seated himself on a log and loudly began to read. His pose was one of elaborate indifference to the kids who came to catch the performance. But, behind the lifted book, I saw his eyes dart up from the page now and then to note his erudition's effect on his awestruck audience.

The scene was, in a way, comical; in another, strangely pathetic. I turned away, feeling not a laugh but a catch in the throat.

This same pride in learning I found all up and down the Urubamba. Especially among the Piros, one of the first tribes SIL tackled. When Townsend wants to give grounds for his great expectations among others, he says, "Take a look at the Piros."

Heroine of the Piro advance is Esther Matteson of Oakland, California. A quiet-spoken young woman with the radiant face of a saint and the firm jaw of an American pioneer woman, she came down with the Townsends shortly after President Prado opened the door, helped survey the tribes, tramping endless miles through matted jungle, helping pole dugout canoes and balsa rafts on exploratory trips through dangerous river rapids.

Esther and a companion went to live with the Piros in 1947; she has been with them ever since. She faced all the usual obstacles—adjusting to primitive living conditions, the Indians' early distrust and hostility, the towering task of learning from scratch a language about which there was no data whatever. Her accomplishments to date:

There are 13 Piro-Spanish schools scattered along the Ucayali, Urubamba, Manu and Acre Rivers, one of them an adult school for tribal teachers. In Esther's schools are 450 children and adults fiercely tackling such subjects as reading, writing, arithmetic, Peruvian history, mechanics and sewing, the rudiments of Spanish. As a result of their education, many Piros now vote regularly in national elections, govern themselves by democratic rules, have title to their own lands, cut and sell timber, grow crops for sale where hitherto they grew them only for their own use, are fast forming an independent society that is a happy blend of the best in their own culture and that of the white man.

One in every three Piros is a Christian. Esther has translated into Piro the entire New Testament, many educational works besides texts, a book of 91 hymns, plus a long list of linguistic and ethnological studies of her tribe for scientific journals.

At a tidy little village called Bufeo Pozo I met 40-year-old Moran Zumaeta, one of Esther Matteson's prize Piro teachers. Moran's hunger for education, he told me, antedated Esther's coming. For years he hammered at every door where he thought "there might be somebody to feed my famished mind." Everywhere he was rebuffed, everywhere told, "Indians can't learn." Finally he stumbled upon Esther, struggling to set up a small school on the Urubamba. She told him, "You not only can learn; you *must*."

In an incredibly short time, with her encouragement he learned to read and write his own language, has become proficient in Spanish and four other tribal tongues.

Moran taught for four years, without pay, at a village named Huau where Esther had begun a school. There he was further trained by government educators, sent to Bufeo Pozo to take charge of the government school there, then to other villages. In his home village, hundreds of miles away, he started a school with his own two sons in a small lean-to; suspicious of his motives, no others would come at first. At the end of nine months he had 34 students, made 31 converts to Christianity.

Everywhere Moran went he inflamed his people with his own boundless yen to learn, multiplied himself by training others to teach. Today he supervises four schools and eight teachers, often travels the dangerous rivers all night to reach his next school by class time.

I sat in the back of Moran's school at Bufeo Pozo, listened to him teach. The room was crowded to capacity, Esther's primers before them. At one desk sat a Piro father and son bent over the same book, at another a mother and daughter eagerly studying together.

Esther's Piro-land is filled with striking stories of Christian transformation. Take Hishonki, for example. After two years on the Urubamba, Esther began translation of Bible verses. To help her, she engaged Hishonki, an eager young student whose only other passion was for fishing. One day while they were laboring over the correct Piro rendering for Christ's word, "Follow me, and I will make you fishers of men," he stopped suddenly to ask, "Teacher, does that apply to me?" Esther replied, "I think it applies especially to you, Hishonki!" He was her first convert, became an evangelist among his own people, within a year had won 200 other Piros to the Christian faith.

Another eminent convert is Chomawari, the Piro chieftain. Chomawari told me he not only "believes with the head" but governs his people by the Bible. The result: morality among the tribe, formerly one of the most licentious in all Peru, is 80 per cent better than it was ten years ago, according to government Indian service officials.

Not long ago, when a rash of misdeeds broke out among his tribe, Chomawari summoned the evil-doers to his house, called in Esther Matteson. "Read what God says about playing with another man's wife," he thundered. Then "Read what God says about witchcraft." Then "Read what God says about drunkenness." With the culprits properly humbled by Holy Writ, Chomawari softened, "I will not punish you," he said, "if God the Great Chief does not. But sin no more!" Later, all the offenders became Christians.

Of all a linguist's tasks, says Cam Townsend, Bible translation is the trickiest. It must be preceded not only by proficiency with the language, but an intimate knowledge of a tribe's customs and taboos as well. "Figures of speech that may be meaningful to one brought up in the Anglo-American tradition are often mystifying booby-traps to a primitive man's understanding."

Some Biblical similes, literally translated, can convey lethal suggestion. For example, one linguist living with tribesmen who had a penchant for burning their enemies bethought himself in time to avoid recommending that they "heap coals of fire on his head." He translated it instead, "Make him ashamed by your friendliness."

The speech of jungle Indians, for all its complexity of syntax, is forthright and to the point. One tribesman, listening to the parable of the fruitless sower who scattered seed on stony ground and among thorns, scoffed indignantly at such stupidity. "Served him right," he said. "Didn't he know enough to dig a hole for the seed like we Indians do?"

Tribal "informants" who help out the linguists are sticklers for a common-sense rendering. A linguist trying out a literal translation of the Sermon on the Mount got only as far as "And he opened his mouth and taught them saying—" when his informant demanded, "How could he talk with his mouth open? To talk, you have to open and close the mouth!" The linguist promptly revised it: "And he began to talk . . ."

Suggestions from the Indians themselves often help to make the wording clearer than in the English Bible. When a tribe was getting nothing from Christ's warning, "If any man offend one of these my little ones . . . ," the translator took an Indian's tip and put the onus on "any man who shows one of these my little ones the wrong path." In another tribal language the same passage is rendered, "If anyone spoils the heart of one of these my little ones."

To the Huanuco Quechuas the phrase "Do not tempt God" meant "Do not entice God to sin"; the translator rendered it, "Don't push God to do what you want." And when the Cashibos puzzled over the phrase, "God is no respecter of persons," their linguist rendered it, "God doesn't just look at the face."

Townsend insists that the great doctrines "must be explained in living, understandable words." Abstract terms are always tough. In some tribes "God's love" is too weak; one tribe describes divine compassion thus: "God hurts in His heart for us." To the Piros such words as "faith" and "believe" are incomplete by themselves; they insist that "believing in God" must also connote action; so they make it "to obey-believe." For the Shipibos "doubt" is described as "thinking two things"; "pride" means "I outrank others." The same tribe makes a covetous person "one who has gone crazy for things." The Piros equate "peace" with "the well-arranged soul." For another tribe the phrase "Our hope is in God" is translated, "We hang onto God."

To Townsend such translations are "an improvement not only for jungle Indians but possibly for modern Americans as well."

After developing a passage as best he can, the linguist tries it out on his tribe, submits it to long discussion, revises it over and over again until the Indians' reaction indicates crystal-clear understanding.

"A single book of the Bible may take years to translate satisfactorily," says Townsend.

Final polishing of Bible translations and school texts is done by SIL linguists at Yarinacocha. Away from the distracting demands of their tribes, in small shacks Townsend built at the base for that purpose, they can huddle for hours with their Indian informants and patiently put together the information from stacks of notes and tape recordings made in the field.

Most Indian informants are also teacher candidates. Thus, bringing them to the base serves a double purpose. Between helping with the translating, they attend classes fitting them to take over the schools started by the linguists.

The government school for teacher-training has become one of the most important activities at Yarinacocha. It got its start some years ago when Townsend took Peruvian educators on a tour of his jungle schools that were being taught by Indians groomed for the job by the linguists. The educators were amazed. "You've laid the groundwork for a whole educational program," they said.

The result: in 1953 the Ministry of Education set up its

Curso de Capacitación Pedagógica at Yarinacocha. Since then, during the first three months of each year, promising tribesmen have been brought in for intensive courses in Spanish, advanced academic subjects, teaching methods. Accredited, they return to their tribes as government-paid teachers and hoist over their jungle schoolhouses the official crest of the Ministry of Education.

In 1958, 75 teacher candidates took the course. Bringing their families with them, many traveled for days by canoe and raft to reach the base, while others came on the Institute's planes. They represented 16 different tribes—"a sort of jungle version of the United Nations," Townsend calls them. While I was at Yarinacocha, someone pointed out a chummy pair of teacher candidates comparing notes and laughing together. "They belong to tribes that have been mortal enemies for generations," said my informant. "Had they met in the jungle a few years ago, they'd have killed each other on sight."

Dr. Morote Best, a brilliant educator, said to me, "Until only a short while ago, nobody could convince me that jungle Indians could learn. Then one day I came upon a pair of these young girl linguists. I could scarcely believe my eyes when I saw their crowded little school, found boys studying books by firelight, older people struggling to learn to read and write. I said to myself, 'There *is* hope for our Indians.'"

Returning to Lima, he gave a glowing account of what he'd seen. "These young North Americans," he said, "are showing us how to cut through the wilderness of ignorance, helping to bring our aborigines into the life of our country. They deserve help."

In January 1957 Dr. Morote was appointed by the Ministry of Education as supervisor of the jungle schools, now has his own thatched house at SIL's jungle base, spends much of his time on inspection swings through the jungles. He shares Cam Townsend's conviction that "the newly educated Indian cannot subsist on his former economy of fishing and hunting. Until recently a semi-nomad, moving from place to place in search of new hunting and fishing grounds, he has been shown the advantages of settling in permanent villages, where his children can go to school and he can make a better life for himself."

To help jungle Indians realize that better life, the Peruvian government has launched a brand-new program to teach modern agricultural methods to the tribes. On land adjoining the SIL base, 250 acres have been set aside where Indian teacher trainees can study agriculture under trained SIL agronomists. To date, 21 teachers have taken the agriculture course, and now are showing their fellow tribesmen how to market their products.

Townsend's aim of "not taking the Indian out of the jungle but taking the jungle out of the Indian" sounds good—to all save those with romantic notions about primitive peoples' bliss in their native state. One day, after a large audience had been told about his work, a hearer arose to bait him with the familiar canard: "You missionaries make me sick! Why force civilization on a people so unspoiled and happy? Why not leave 'em alone!"

Townsend replied, laughing, "I think, my friend, you've been no closer to jungle Indians than the movies. If you could sit down with them, as I have, and hear them tell in their own tongues the woes that haunt them through witchcraft, superstition, fear and strife; listen to mothers tell of being forced to strangle their newborn babies because of some evil omen; see old folks being abandoned to die because they had become a burden; or sense the hatreds bred in them by generations of white men who took advantage of their ignorance to exploit them, steal their lands, ravage their women and ruthlessly shoot them down—well, then, my friend, you just might change your mind about Indians as a quaint people living lives of idyllic happiness."

Townsend's position is, "Sooner or later, whether we like it or not, civilization is going to come to these tribes. Our concern is that it be *Christian* civilization."

Not so concerned are those who make their living from oppressing the Indians. Some of the *patrones*, for example. These look sourly upon anybody who would educate the Indians, encourage them to own their own property, work their own lands, vote for their rights. Not infrequently one of them will complain to the government, lift false bogeymen against SIL. Generally, however, they get short shrift from officials who know better.

When, a few years ago, a wealthy *patrón* charged Townsend's people with being "foreigners who cunningly work close to our country's borders, smuggle in goods from the States to undersell us," his plaint was promptly filed in the wastebasket.

Governments normally indifferent or even hostile to Christian mission endeavor of the usual kind welcome SIL with open arms. And that despite the fact that Townsend makes no bones about SIL's ultimate goal—to put the Bible in every tribe, in its own tongue.

To detractors of such a goal, Townsend replies forth-rightly, "Of *course* that's what we are aiming at. But don't forget that on the way to that goal, our workers pacify savage tribes, awaken ambition in Indians, prepare them for integration into the life of your country—to which, in time, they will make a big contribution."

Townsend is equally deft in parrying thrusts from another quarter—the religious. Such attacks are rare, since SIL's members represent no religious body, coöperate with all. There was, however, the time in 1953 when a Lima news-paper carried a series of articles by a prominent Roman Catholic blasting SIL workers as "Protestant wolves," their work "sectarian and proselyting in nature," and demanding their expulsion. Townsend ignored the first blast. When others followed, he composed a letter to the editor which one Catholic authority applauded as "a masterpiece of Chris-tian love and reconciliation."

Townsend wrote in part: "It is not a question of 'wolves.' Every SIL member must promise that his service will be given in a spirit of love and brotherhood, without distinction as to race or creed. We do not call ourselves Protestants but simply believers in Christ, and because of our nonsectarian nature we do not teach rituals and ecclesiastical systems.

"While we are motivated by the desire to serve God and humanity, we are at the same time scientists dedicated to the study of languages. And when we complete our lin-guistic investigations we shall go, leaving behind our base at Yarinacocha, with all its buildings, for a center of Indian education."

The letter was prominently displayed in the newspaper.

The attacks ceased, and Townsend and his workers went on with their comradely friendship with Roman Catholic missionaries stationed in the jungles: gladly transporting them back and forth to their posts, repairing their radios, sharing medical supplies, bringing them to Yarinacocha for outings. The priests and nuns have responded in kind, performing innumerable acts of neighborly helpfulness to SIL workers. Both groups agree that "the jungle," in Townsend's words, "is too big and too needy for anybody there to quarrel with anybody else."

This year the Papal Nuncio in Lima, cordially receiving Townsend, asked God's blessing upon his work "after listening most graciously to how we hope to attain our goal of putting Holy Writ into 2000 more languages in this generation."

I asked Townsend his chances of attaining that goal. Since SIL is thus far at work among "only" 175 of the 2000 language groups, would he have to revise his estimate of the time it will take? Townsend's reply is the measure of his spirit.

"Not a bit," he said. "Consider the tempo of our advance. In 1942 we were at work in only one country; today we're in 12. Since 1942 our increase of workers has been 1600 percent. At that rate our membership will number more than 12,000 in 15 years. That should do it!"

I began to understand why the late Josephus Daniels, then U.S. Ambassador to Mexico, had called Townsend "a man with the most audacious faith I ever knew."

Surely no project is built more completely on faith. From the time that he and Leonard Legters, SIL's co-founder, decided to emulate Abram in trusting God even to "going out, not knowing whither," Townsend's guiding principle has been, "Go nowhere God doesn't lead; go anywhere He does."

But, I asked, how can one determine what is God's leading and what may be merely the nudge of one's own desire? To Townsend it is profoundly simple: "We simply take our inner urges to God in prayer, saying, 'If this is Thy will, not ours alone, open the way.' Then if support comes, we know that the door has not been jimmied by our will but has been opened by God's hand."

If such dependence upon the divine sounds silly, improvident—well, that's the way God set it up. Just another indication that He knows how man's heart can play tricks sometimes, crossing the wires, and needs to be told, "Lean not to thine own understanding." And just another evidence that "The foolishness of God is wiser than man."

Townsend does not campaign for funds in the usual ways, even with an annual budget which exceeds a million dollars. He says, "I have never asked a man directly for a dollar and I never shall." To him, the wheedling of gifts from reluctant givers is not only a denial of trust in God; it's an offense to the dignity of God's work, and does little for the giver. "We like our givers to be God-inspired partners, not badgered Lady Bountifuls."

His practice of waiting for God's go-ahead, with funds providentially provided, permeates the whole SIL organization. No member is salaried. There is no guaranteed allowance. Each is expected to "look to the Lord" to stir the hearts of interested people to support his work—without the worker himself lifting a syllable in direct request. "Give full information without solicitation," Townsend tells SIL members. To this he adds the rider, "Even the information should be given in such a way that the hearers will realize that our full expectation is in God and not man."

Getting enthusiastic coöperation for his SIL program is another mark of the Townsend genius. "We do not go into any country nowadays," he says, "without being invited." True; but he shows a remarkable talent for getting invited. He spends much time frequenting conferences where educators and officials discuss their indigenes and what to do about them. Mingling with the experts, he quietly tells what SIL has accomplished elsewhere. As in Mexico, Peru and Ecuador, he has not had to wangle permission to enter; they invite him in—fast, with full government coöperation.

In tribute to his work with their people, Latin-American nations have showered Townsend with kudos. Colleges and universities seek him as lecturer, have tried to load him with honorary degrees—most of which he has respectfully declined. The president of Peru has decorated him with the Order of Merit for Distinguished Service, rarely accorded to non-Peruvians. The government of Ecuador has conferred upon him the Decoration of Merit, acclaiming him "spiritual conqueror of the jungle."

But the tribute that has moved him most came from an Indian chief in the Amazonian jungle, whose tribe he and his SIL had transformed with hope. Said the chief, "Before you came, there was only darkness. Now there is only light."

VII

Bolivia's Most Unforgettable Character

One afternoon a few years ago an American of some self-importance strode into the crowded *Clínica Americana,* a Methodist mission hospital in La Paz, the capital of Bolivia. Brushing past a line of patiently waiting Indians, the visitor exclaimed: "Who's in charge here? I am——" and he mentioned a name well known in the entertainment world.

A tall, spare man arose slowly from bandaging an Indian child's leg. "And *I,*" he said, "am Dr. Beck. Take your place at the end of the line, please."

This story, repeated with relish in La Paz, sharply limns the character of the missionary doctor known throughout Latin-America as "the father of modern medicine in Bolivia."

Back in 1912, when Frank Beck first came to Bolivia, the country's 750,000 Aymara Indians were among the most neglected and depressed peoples on earth. Though they comprised one third of Bolivia's population they had no schools, no political rights, no health provisions. They were virtual slaves, bought and sold as part of farms or industries where they worked. Today, largely because of Dr. Beck's labors, the Aymaras have made an impressive start toward a place in the sun.

156

I had not been in La Paz an hour before I understood why this remarkable American has been named "the outstanding foreigner in Bolivia."

"You know Dr. Beck?" I asked a traffic policeman. "*Sí, sí, señor,*" he beamed. "Does not everyone?"

In broken English he told how Beck had delivered his baby, worked until almost dawn to save his wife's life, then spent hours driving him about to spread the tidings among his numerous kin. "Ah, *señor,*" said the cop, "there's a man who leaves his mark on you!"

For more than four decades Frank Beck has been leaving his mark on Bolivians, first as teacher, then as doctor. Many of the country's leaders have either studied under him or received his medical ministrations, often both.

President Hernan Siles Zuazo, a former student of Beck in the American Institute, told me, "He awakened us to our responsibility to human beings as human beings. Can you understand what that means to the future of Bolivia?"

Among missionaries he is a shining example of that vast company of the dedicated who cannot rest until they have left behind all of life's comforts and gone to earth's end to serve their fellow man.

Frank Beck's sharp gray eyes first scanned far horizons while he was a student at Dakota Wesleyan University. A roommate named John Washburn went to teach at the American Institute in La Paz (founded in 1907 by Methodist missions) and wrote back: "If you're looking for a place to invest your life, Frank, this is it!"

Excitedly Beck talked it over with a pert junior named Bessie Dunn, daughter of a Methodist preacher from Iowa. In 1912, freshly possessed of his college diploma, he accepted a teaching post at the American Institute in Cochabamba, just established as one of a growing string of Methodist schools in South America. A year later Bessie arrived at the port of Mollendo, Peru. "Guess we'll have to be married here," Frank told her. "Spanish custom doesn't permit a single woman to travel unchaperoned!" They were married by the mayor of Mollendo. During the ceremony Bessie became so entranced by the flowery Spanish flourishes that Frank had to nudge her and whisper, "It's time to say *si*, Bessie." They made the 10-day trip into Bolivia's interior by train, boat, dugout canoe and mule-cart across the Andes.

In 1914 the Becks were sent to Buenos Aires to help start *Colegio Ward*, now one of the most famous schools in Latin America. They lived in a tent on the campus so that the apartment provided for them could be rented to raise funds for needy students. In 1917 they went back to Bolivia, and in 1920 Beck was appointed director of the thriving American Institute in La Paz.

It was three years later that Frank Beck came to a decision that had long been building in him: he would switch his field of service from education to medicine. He had been increasingly haunted by the dark image of a potentially great people, the Aymaras, shuffling through life with physical maladies, dying before their time, with the social and political cards hopelessly stacked against them.

In miserable hovels on the city fringes and out upon the high plateau above La Paz, thousands of Indian families had never known a doctor. Infant mortality was as high as 80 per cent. In La Paz there was only the poorly equipped municipal hospital.

When his mission board back in the United States encouraged him to change his career, Beck announced that he would take a furlough and put himself through medical school. Returning to Chicago with Mrs. Beck and their two children, he enrolled at Northwestern University's medical school at the age of 35. Five years later, by tutoring on the side, he had completed his medical work and was interning at the Indianapolis Methodist Hospital.

In October 1928 he and his family headed back to Bolivia and, after he served as a traveling doctor for a year, he set up shop in a tumble-down shed near the American Institute. His equipment: three rickety beds, an old pressure cooker for a sterilizer and a $35 set of instruments, discards from World War I.

One of his first patients was an Aymara woman in a condition of eclampsia labor—an attack of convulsions usually fatal in that area. While curious Indian faces stared through the window, he managed to save both mother and baby. This was the first of some 4000 successful maternity cases which in 25 years completely changed the attitude of Bolivian doctors and public on the importance of obstetrical care. In those days few women called in doctors at childbirth.

As word of his skill got around, the little clinic became crowded. It was not uncommon to see a bejeweled ambassador's wife next to a colorfully garbed Indian woman. To reach Indians who would not or could not come to the clinic, he made trips on a sputtery motorcycle out on the Altiplano, sloshing through mud and wading hip-deep rivers to get to his unwilling patients.

He found conditions beyond his worst dreams: obstetrical cases botched by widwives or witch-doctors, every variety of cancer, hernia, ulcer, kidney and liver trouble. Whole families lived in unventilated, damp, one-room huts where even the mildest infirmities often became fatal. Because of the high altitude, whooping cough was especially deadly among children.

At first the Indians, distrustful of any white man's intentions, refused to come close to this lanky gringo and his magic medicine. But his persistent friendliness, plus his talent for performing "miracles" of healing, in time won them over.

There was, for instance, the Aymara woman who had been gored by a bull. Almost completely disemboweled, her intestines were hanging out when Beck got to her. To an obbligato of her groans and wailing by the pueblo people, a witch-doctor was uttering loud incantations and feverishly slapping on herbs and leaves. Almost by force, Beck took the woman back to his clinic, sewed her up, and in two weeks she was back home. The people gaped in unbelief. "Why she not die?" they exclaimed. "Everything all on outside, now all inside!"

As a result, more and more Aymaras came trudging into the clinic, or brought their sick to mutely lay before him along roads and rivers where he was known to come.

Dr. Beck asked no pay of the Aymaras. In their gratitude, however, they sometimes put a chicken or a few eggs or ears of corn on his clinic doorstep or on the seat of his motorcycle side-car.

The medical profession in La Paz, what there was of it, gave him a hard time at first. They did not relish this outlander coming in to take patients from whom they could exact exorbitant fees. They liked even less his acting as though Indians' lives counted. His temporary license to practice was alternately revoked and renewed for years. But he went right on practicing, license or no license.

In 1932, with a war being waged between Bolivia and Paraguay, Beck was asked to provide medical assistance for the Bolivian Army. The war was fought in a disease-cursed jungle area called the Gran Chaco—more realistically dubbed "the Green Hell." Soldiers died like flies from tuberculosis, malaria, instestinal infections. Beck, burning with malaria himself, fought to save casualties of both germs and bullets. He could operate only between four and six o'clock in the morning, after the clouds of mosquitoes had dispersed and before swarms of vicious gnats took over. For his unsparing labors during the fighting he was awarded the "Condor of the Andes," the highest honor that is ever given to foreigners.

In 1935, desperate to expand his 15-bed hospital, Beck gambled most of his meager funds on a trip to the United States to seek building money. When none was available from his mission board, he sought individual donors, and finally reached Mr. and Mrs. Henry Pfeiffer of the Hudnut family. Before them he spread out photographs, talked steadily for 15 minutes. Mrs. Pfeiffer finally halted him to say quietly, "We'll give you $30,000."

Jubilantly, he returned to La Paz and began construction on a suburban site. To stretch his capital he pitched in himself, pushing wheelbarrows of cement, doing all the wiring. To friends who marveled at his mechanical resourcefulness, he replied that if he had his way every missionary would be born and raised on a farm. "What I learned on the farm has been more important to me as a missionary doctor than much that I learned at medical school," he said. When his building fund ran low he invited local mine-owners and businessmen to send their employees for treatment, asked for construction help in return. Receiving a small inheritance from his father, he threw it into the project, as well as every spare dollar he could find from any source.

Meanwhile, Beck kept up a barrage of appeals to friends back home. From a man in Montclair, New Jersey, came an electric generator for use during power failures; from a woman in Pittsburgh an elevator. American and British residents of La Paz contributed furniture, an oxygen tent, an incubator, an inhalator. When the hospital was completed it was the most modern in Bolivia, capable of handling 80 patients.

Beck's particular pride was the home and school for 30 nurses. When he had arrived in Bolivia, nursing as a profession was virtually unknown. Young women with education sufficient to qualify for training (mostly Spanish, from wealthy families) scorned nursing as "servant work." To get the necessary technical personnel, Beck brought in underprivileged girls, imbued them with the idea that here was a chance at a professional life not otherwise open to them, then rigidly drilled them in the arts of healing.

By 1955 the nursing school of *Clínica Americana* had turned out 103 graduates. Today hospitals, health centers and clinics throughout Latin America clamor for nurses trained there. At one time the public-health section of *Servicio Cooperativo Interamericano*, U.S. foreign-aid agency, had 34 Beck-trained nurses on its staff, declared them "the best in the world."

Dr. Beck is gratified by such accolades, but even more by the fact that the Bolivian government is closely copying his nurse-training program in its public health service. He says: "The biggest contribution that medical missions can make is to stimulate others to do for themselves."

At *Clínica Americana,* mornings were for operations— often as many as six a day; afternoons for out-patient consultations, which averaged 7400 a year. Beck's charge to all was 1000 bolivianos (about 20¢)—if his patients had it. On Wednesday afternoons, his only time off duty, he visited La Paz orphanages to conduct clinics, perform minor operations, bandage up wounds, making no charge to either patient or institution.

Beck's nurses said of him, "Only God could be more omnipresent." From the first he insisted on living in a small apartment on the clinic's top floor where he could hear every night sound, tell by a nurse's step down the corridor whether he was needed. "When you're trying to *do* a job," he said, "you've got to be *on* the job." Told he would kill himself by overwork, he snorted: "Work doesn't kill a man; worry does."

Bed patients soon learned to detect his short, quick step in the corridors, were comforted by his habit of softly singing hymns, humming or whistling as he performed operations. One, asked if her emergency appendectomy was an ordeal, replied, "How could it be? The señor doctor's voice was more soothing than the anesthetic."

Between clinical chores in La Paz, Beck continued his trips to the Altiplano to conduct wayside clinics, deliver babies, take out teeth, patch up broken bones, pep-talk the people into better self-health measures.

Some time ago a delegation of Indians tramped four days to ask Beck to start a school at Ancoraimes, on beautiful Lake Titicaca. Their children needed both education and medi-

cine. "How else," asked their spokesman, "can we help our
people to a better life?"

Next day, Beck mounted his motorcycle, its side-car packed
with tools, nails, rough siding. The Indians helped him throw
up a one-room structure, then spread the word that education
had at long last come to Ancoraimes.

When school opened, Aymara children were present in
droves. School had no sooner begun than the town's mayor
appeared, trailing a cordon of police. Beck was thrown into
jail, spent the night fuming in his cell. In court the next day,
he indignantly addressed the magistrate. "They say I have
no right to start a school here, or vaccinate your children
against smallpox. What in humanity's name . . ."

The judge smiled and lifted a hand. "You don't remember
me, Dr. Beck? I studied under you at the American Institute!" He called the authorities to the bench, made them
apologize. Then, turning to Beck, he said: "Please teach us
better manners toward our benefactors."

Today, as a result of Beck's help, there are 18 Methodist
schools on Titicaca's shores, plus a small clinic and a four-
room cottage for the doctor. The schools and clinic serve
26,000 Indians, who come from 35 miles around. The settlement is named "Beck Memorial."

Political revolutions in Bolivia occur with whimsical regu-
larity. During his 44 years there, Beck survived many. Never
taking sides, he deplored them mainly for their inevitable
dumping of wounded on his doorstep. When he saw an
upheaval coming, he alerted his staff, then took care of the
casualties as they came, with no regard to the side they
represented.

After one unusually violent upset some years back, an officer of the successful *coup* stamped into the clinic to demand preferred treatment for his patriots. Beck grabbed his arm and marched him outside—fast. "I'm in command here," he said firmly. "Go!"

During the 1944 revolution, a cocky young soldier burst into the clinic. "It is believed you have fugitives here," he boomed. "I search!" Amused, Beck led him gravely through the wards, only slightly discomforted by the sub-machine gun the boy carelessly waved in his face. Beck was about to open the last door when the soldier lowered his gun, accidentally tripped the trigger, and blew off half his own toe. Enraged that anyone would so carelessly endanger his patients, Beck escorted the soldier to surgery and took off the rest of his toe—without benefit of anesthetic.

To Bolivian politicians, this blunt but courageous American was at first an enigma, then a delight. Almost every regime has sought his counsel, wanting to know what he thought of their policies. "Dr. Beck," a prominent leader informed me, "always gives it to us straight, as you Americans say. It's refreshing—and helpful. He's been more of a political power than he realizes. For he thinks with his heart."

When the Siles government came to power in 1952, sweeping land reforms were initiated. Indians, for the first time in 400 years, now own their own land, are able to negotiate wages. In June of 1956 they were given the right to vote, something hitherto unknown in Bolivia's long history. Though Beck thought the reforms went too fast and too far, they dramatically reflected his long striving for the rights of the oppressed.

Early in 1956 Frank Beck announced his retirement and

return to the United States. It was his third try at leaving the clinic and the people he loved. The first was in 1944 when, suffering from arthritis of the spine, he was told he would have to quit the high altitude. But, after seven months in the States, word reached him that the burden had proved too much for his successor. Beck hustled back to his clinic.

His second try at retirement was in 1950. A Texas mining concern promptly offered him a job at $12,000 a year—a handsome sum for a man whose salary as a missionary had not averaged above $750 a year, on which he and Mrs. Beck had educated three of their own and two adopted children. But he turned it down to serve with the Associated Medical Missions office in New York, charged with certifying missionary doctors. For two years he chafed under the desk routine, brooded over how things were going in La Paz. Then his second successor also resigned under the strain—and once again he happily headed back to Bolivia.

Before his last retirement, Dr. Beck took the precaution of having his passport stamped with the "*reingreso*" visa, permitting him to return at any time. "Just in case," he said with a grin.

The Becks were given a royal send-off, with many speeches. U.S. Ambassador Gerald A. Drew asserted: "I have served in many countries, but in none has one man done so much to benefit the people of a land not his own."

An Aymara chieftain said simply: "He brought my people back to life."

Frank Beck wound up his 44 years in Bolivia typically. On the day of his departure, there were five operations to be done. One of the last was performed on a 3-year-old Indian boy whose tongue, horribly tumored and projecting inches from his mouth, had to be removed to save his life. The child being an orphan, Beck had arranged for his 6-year-old sister to stay in the room with him. After the operation he found her there, one small brown hand smoothing the child's forehead, while bravely she struggled to hold back the tears streaming down her face.

I watched as Dr. Beck gathered the little form into his arms, heard him say gently, over and over: *Estará bien, mama pequeña"* . . . "It's going to be all right, little mother. It's going to be all right."

In essence, this has been Frank Beck's lifelong message to Bolivia's poor and oppressed.

All over Latin America thousands today will affirm that he went a far way toward making the promise come true.

VIII

One Man Against "Apartheid"

One September day in 1943 a 29-year-old priest of the Church of England stepped off a ship into a South Africa aboil with race tensions. Less than three years before, handsome Trevor Huddleston, scion of a noted British family, had taken his vows in an Anglican monastic order called the Community of the Resurrection, whose members are committed to bring to bear upon society the social implications of the Christian gospel.

Those implications were sorely needed in the Union of South Africa, a fiery caldron of rising hatreds between the country's two and a half million whites and ten million non-whites. Busily stoking the flames was the Nationalist Party leader who would become Prime Minister in 1948, Dr. Daniel F. Malan, to whom white made right and whose twin slogans were: "Africa for the Afrikanders" and "Keep the Kaffir in his place." Malan's formula for achieving both aims was *apartheid,* meaning race separation, and pronounced, significantly, "apart-hate."

Huddleston's appointment was to Sophiatown, a black township in the city of Johannesburg. His mission station was the one that novelist Alan Paton used as a setting for his 1948 best-seller, *Cry, the Beloved Country.* The young priest was appalled when he saw *apartheid* at work. Johannesburg's white suburbs were lovely with beautiful homes and gardens; its areas reserved for blacks were bleak, crowded shanty-towns.

The color bar was high and forbidding; one could cross it only at the risk of his life. Natives moved about knee-deep in restrictions. Signs were up everywhere, sorting the two races like an efficient machine. By day the native could mine the white man's gold, wash his dishes, tend his garden, mind his babies, empty his garbage cans. But at night the races separated, one half proceeding to lovely homes in the suburbs, the other to squalid shelters in the slums.

Apartheid, often enforced by police clubs, was breeding envy, resentment and hatred in frightening proportions. One sign at a street crossing was symptomatic: it had been amended to read "Natives *Very* Cross Here!" And Johannesburg's white citizens recognized the hatred by bolting their houses at night, sleeping with revolvers under their pillows. That first evening in Johannesburg, Huddleston prayed with fierce intensity: "God, give me strength to fight this evil thing!"

His crusade to break the shackles of Africans soon made him a target for the revilings of racists. Frequently termed an agitator, he replied quietly, "The Christian is always, if true to his calling, an agitator." But the blacks, with whom he was to live for 12 years, called him *Makhalipile*—"dauntless one." Soon the tall, spare figure striding through Sophia-town, his cassock whipping about his long legs and a clutch of youngsters at his heels, became a familiar sight.

From the first he resolved to identify himself completely with the people of Sophiatown, their struggles, their hopes and dreams. He did not think of them as black—but as *people*. Their response was immediate. They flocked to his church. His compassion for them matched his indignation at their treatment. He knew that morality and integrity were not easy virtues in a society which denied all chance for human dignity. It disturbed him to hear himself giving counsel that "I know I could not follow in the same circumstances." Yet, despite all that made goodness difficult to achieve, he saw his people taking on spiritual stature.

His indignation flamed one day when he heard a Dutch Reformed Church leader assert that "mixed worship would scarcely be edifying." The word rankled in his heart as he went that evening to hear confessions. He noted in his diary, "Old Martha is beside me now. She used to work in a white kitchen, but cannot now because of her arthritis. Her hands, calloused from work in the white man's kitchen, and gnarled with arthritis, are clasping a prayer book. I kneel with her—and indeed I am not 'edified.' I only want to kneel and wash those old and weary feet!"

Of all the restrictions spawned by *apartheid*, none got Huddleston's dander so high as the pass laws. To go anywhere, any time, the native must carry a pass. Easy to lose or misplace—and reissue made difficult by the deliberate procrastination of officials—the pass is the native's slender right to freedom. To be without it is a crime punishable by fine or imprisonment, often by police brutality, and sometimes death.

Of some 75,000 Negroes jailed each year in Johannesburg, approximately two thirds are pass-law offenders. Trials average less than two minutes each. "Pass-law crimes require no docket to be opened, no witness to be questioned, no statements to be taken," a police official explains. "Non-production of a pass, or a pass out of order, is generally proof in itself that an offense has been committed."

Father Huddleston was soon devoting much of his precious time and scant mission funds to helping pass-violators. An employe or schoolboy at his mission would disappear. Nine times out of ten he would be found in jail—thrown in with hardened crooks, drug addicts, murderers, simply because he'd left his pass at home.

Often a pass was no deterrent to police wanting to impress their authority on a native. One morning Father Huddleston found Jonas, one of his schoolboys, in the jail yard, charged with vagrancy. "Where was your pass?" he asked. "They tore it up," the boy replied. The priest stormed into the police station, found the torn pass in the waste-basket. When he refused to surrender it, he himself was arrested. A few days later the prison commandant apologized —to Huddleston, not to Jonas.

Many pass-law cases ended tragically, particularly if a native defended himself in any manner that could be regarded as "cheeky." On one occasion, one of Father Huddleston's flock died of a bladder injury after being kicked in the stomach by police. The priest went to court with affidavits from two doctors stating the nature of the injury. The magistrate brushed him off. The verdict: the man died of "congenital syphilis."

Huddleston saw that the pass laws caused more crime than they curbed. The Africans reasoned: "If it's a crime to be in the street without a bit of paper, and if that crime is punished with a fine or imprisonment, why not commit a crime that's worth while?" Consequently, Johannesburg has one of the highest crime rates in the world, and black Johannesburg is largely ruled by criminals.

To help beat back crime's rising tide in Sophiatown, Father Huddleston addressed himself to what police call "the No. 1 problem in urban Africa"—the *tsotsis*. These are teen-age gangs who terrorized the streets with stabbings, rapes, robberies. Huddleston, convinced that the high rate of youth crime was greatly encouraged by the lack of recreational facilities, started a club for the *tsotsis*, enrolled them as acolytes in his church. His rooms were "open house" where youngsters could come to read magazines, talk out their hopes and fears.

When the Community of the Resurrection offered the city council seven acres of church property for use as an African recreation center, a white vigilance committee moved in fast to defeat the project. Undismayed, Father Huddleston wrote a letter to the *Rand Daily Mail*, pointing out: "There are 12 public swimming pools and 3000 private pools in Johannesburg for whites—but none for Africans."

He boldly appealed for funds to build a pool at Orlando, a jam-packed Negro "location" near Sophiatown. It took him three years to raise the money, but when the pool was opened 3000 Africans were on hand, and 600 black youngsters leaped in, clothes and all, shouting and splashing. Thenceforth delinquency took a sharp dive in that area.

He used the newspapers to call attention to another problem: the vast amount of starvation ("which we euphemistically call 'malnutrition'") among African children. He wrote: "Every white child is entitled to a free meal at school which costs the state sixpence a day. African kids get nothing." The next day he was deluged with offers of food, clothes, money.

Ultimately his pressure—along with the help of a small group of concerned European women—resulted in the feeding scheme being extended to all African schools, at the rate of twopence per day per head. Wryly he commented on "the strange anomaly of well-to-do European children receiving a free meal at three times the value of that allowed an African child," but went ahead setting up centers in every Negro township and "location" until his project was feeding 5000 children a day.

A new field beckoned one day when he discovered a 14-year-old boy, inspired by a Louis Armstrong record, wistfully pining for a trumpet. Wangling an instrument from a music shop, he persuaded an African trumpeter to give the youngster lessons. Then, remembering a visiting musician's statement that "Jazz bands first breached the color bar in the United States," he begged and cajoled other instruments for what became known as the "Huddleston Jazz Band."

He also formed a musical society in Sophiatown, and encouraged top African artists to share their talents with his people. And whenever a distinguished white artist played in Johannesburg, Huddleston asked him to come to Sophiatown. After Yehudi Menuhin had given a concert in his mission, Huddleston noted in his diary: "A door was opened, and my Africans marched through it into a new and entrancing world of sound."

The Johannesburg ban against entertaining colored people in hotels or white homes was an evil which Huddleston turned to good. Africans or Asians of note—artists, statesmen, lecturers—traveling through Johannesburg were welcomed at the mission, where they readily entertained his Africans.

In 1954 the Malan government issued a death edict for Sophiatown. By an accident of history Sophiatown was one of the few South African townships where natives had freehold tenure—the right to own their own homes. The area had its shantytown regions, caused by packing 70,000 people into space suited for 30,000; but it also had miles of little red-roofed homes lining tree-shaded streets. Huddleston had encouraged his people to improve their homes, dreaming of turning the area into a model African suburb. But native-owned homes were a denial of *apartheid*. So, under the excuse of "slum clearance," the Western Areas Resettlement Act condemned the township to be razed. The natives would be sent to an area where freehold tenure did not exist.

February 10, 1955, was Removal Day. The streets were filled with 2000 police and military lorries loading the people's pathetic belongings. Huddleston stood helplessly with his people, watching—and weeping. "I do not weep for the destruction of the material," he wrote that day, "but because we Christians of Johannesburg have failed so utterly to uphold principle against prejudice, the rights of persons against the claims of power."

In April 1955 the government dealt Huddleston and all Christian mission schools an even bigger defeat. With the passage of the Bantu Education Act, all schools were put under state control. For 100 years Christian missionaries had pioneered in education for Africans; nearly every African who could read or write had been educated in a mission school. But the mission schools had made one fatal error: they had taught the black man that he, too, was a child of

God, who made "of one blood all the nations of the earth." The Minister of Native Affairs, H. F. Verwoerd, charged in the Senate: "The mission schools' curriculum and educational practice, by ignoring *apartheid*, have been unable to prepare the native for service within the Bantu community." The mission control of schools, therefore, would have to go.

By now Father Huddleston, as provincial of his Community's order in South Africa, was also superintendent of St. Peter's, a secondary boarding school for natives. Known as the "Black Eton of South Africa," with many distinguished alumni, St. Peter's was his pride. His dilemma was: Should St. Peter's continue under the new regime, teaching a syllabus it considered un-Christian? Or was "Bantu education" better than no education, as some religious leaders argued? Father Huddleston decided on "death with honor." St. Peter's would close.

Huddleston's chief sorrow today is not that he lost so many of his battles against *apartheid* but that he had so little help from his fellow Christians. To Afrikander leaders of the Dutch Reformed Church, which has not only supported *apartheid* but attempted to find a Biblical basis for it, he once sighed, "The truth is, gentlemen, that we seem to worship different Gods."

Among churchmen of his own and other denominations he has spoken out like a cymbal among the flutes. "It is my considered opinion," he says, "that unless the Christian Church in South Africa really faces this issue honestly, within the next generation or less it may well lose—and deservedly—the allegiance of the African people."

Under the present regime, any African asking for equal-

ity of opportunity and a measure of justice and brotherhood
is dubbed a Communist. It pains Huddleston to see Communism "getting official credit for the most elementary ideals
of Christian democracy." Therein he sees a clear and present danger. "Will it be too surprising," he asks, "if Africans
become more and more curious about Communism as more
and more of their expressions of hope are labeled Com-
munistic?"

For all his defeats, Huddleston saw hope in the slow
stirring of the conscience of whites. One day his telephone
rang and a voice said: "You don't know me, Father. I'm
a South African of the third generation, so I suppose I have
all the usual prejudices. But could you use £100 for your
work?" And there were many others like him. Also, increasingly heavy mail came in from unnamed whites who wrote:
"Keep up the good work, Father!"

Were all these people merely salving an uneasy conscience?
"Perhaps in some cases," he said. "But I believe there lies
behind their action a deeper meaning—the same which
drove Nicodemus out into the night to visit the Galilean
Prophet."

Early in 1956 his Community recalled him to England
to take charge of the training of novices, many of whom
had entered the order because of his example. The order
felt that Huddleston, in the face of almost insurmountable
barriers, could accomplish more outside the country.

Before leaving, Huddleston sat in the now-empty St.
Peter's and wrote a book, *Naught for Your Comfort*, which,
with rare eloquence, told the story of his 12 years in South
Africa.

His Africans gave him a send-off such as had seldom been seen in black Johannesburg. Proud in their new uniforms, his "Huddleston Jazz Band" played for him. Speeches and tributes were voiced by African leaders. Afterward, many of his people came up to seize his hand and kiss it. Everywhere voices were lifted in the African goodbye: *"Hamba kahle, Makhalipile"*—"Go well, dauntless one!"

When his departure became known in government circles, Johannes Strijdom, who succeeded Malan as Prime Minister in 1954, is said to have exclaimed, "Well, thank God, that's the last we'll hear of him!"

Mr. Strijdom was never more wrong.

IX

Medicine Man on the Amazon

The little white launch swerved out of the Amazon mainstream and headed up a narrow tributary. Bravely flying a pennant depicting a hand holding a torch aloft, it brushed jungle growth on both sides. At the helm sat a stocky man whose keen eyes searched the occasional clearings along the banks. Suddenly, from a thatched hut a woman ran out, frantically waving a towel. The helmsman nosed the boat's prow into the bank, grabbed a black bag and leaped ashore.

In the hut a man lay screaming in agony. He had just been bitten in the foot by a dreaded bushmaster, deadliest of all Amazonia's snakes. Neighbors were hastily building a fire, preparing to burn the foot until it was completely charred—usual treatment for snakebite in that remote region. The man from the boat hastily loaded a syringe with antivenin, made an injection—and saved another life.

This was Leo Halliwell, an American missionary with a unique ministry. He had no medical degree, not even a pharmacist's certificate, yet for 25 years he carried modern medicine to the Amazon Valley's neglected inhabitants. Steering his aquatic clinic up and down the 1000-mile stretch of river between Belém and Manaus, covering some 12,000 miles a year, Halliwell treated more than a quarter of a million Brazilians and Indians for a host of tropical and other dis-

178

eases. He also gave some 50,000 smallpox vaccinations, handed out literally tons of medicines and unguents, patched up thousands of accident victims.

Best of all, he helped awaken the Brazilian government to the fact that of the region's many rich resources its people are the most important; their health may well decide whether Amazonia's fabulous potential is to be developed or left dormant.

During his youth in Kearney, Nebraska, the notion of being a missionary never crossed Leo Halliwell's mind. With a talent for mechanical tinkering, he studied electrical engineering at the state university. But one day, four years after graduation, he heard exciting stories told by a missionary to Peru. On impulse he applied to the Seventh-day Adventist mission board. In short order he and his graduate-nurse bride, Jessie, were on their way to Bahia, Brazil.

In Bahia the mission leaders soon found they had a recruit steaming with energy, imagination, ingenuity. "Just looking for latitude," he would say when asked why he so restlessly sought new fields. Ample latitude was provided when, in 1929, he was asked to pioneer the mission's work in north Brazil.

The Halliwells realized how huge was their new field when they reached Belém, near the Amazon's 207-mile-wide mouth. Their parish included the whole Amazon basin, almost as big as the continent of Europe.

The Amazon itself was awesome: so deep that transatlantic steamers can go up it for 2300 miles, so wide that one must go 400 miles farther before it narrows to the width of the Mississippi at its mouth. And feeding into it is a mesh of more than 500 tributaries, many of them more than 1000 miles long. Strung out along these endless waterways live two million people: an estimated 300,000 are Stone Age Indians, the rest a racial amalgam of Portuguese, Negro, Indian.

In Belém the Halliwells held evangelistic meetings, visited from house to house, made a few converts, got a small school going. But amid this work with city Brazilians, Halliwell was increasingly haunted by the thought of the unreached river people. Many were descendants of the hordes of adventurers who had flocked in during the rubber boom of 1900–12 and were now left stranded in this immense backwater to eke out their precarious tenure in the jungle wilds. To make matters worse, it was said, they bred like flies—and many of their offspring lived about as long.

After a few months in Belém, Halliwell went up the Amazon by river boat and canoe to see his outlying parishioners. He was dismayed by the people's poverty and superstition, especially by their disease. Their strength was sapped by malaria and malnutrition; their lives were shortened by smallpox, syphilis, leprosy; their existence was threatened by poisonous snakes, alligators, jaguars and other beasts; there wasn't a doctor in all the jungle wilderness.

To Jessie he said, "Isn't it one of our Adventist tenets that 'medical work is the right arm of the Gospel'?" She nodded, and he vowed, "I'm going to give that arm some exercise!"

He used his 1930 furlough in the United States for a six-month course in tropical diseases. Jessie brushed up on midwifery, nutrition, sanitation. They talked before church groups and collected money for their "Amazon adventure."

Back in Brazil, Leo sketched a design for a shallow-draft, 30-foot boat with a 10-foot beam. He hacked out the hull by hand from Amazon hardwoods and installed the engine and wiring himself. He christened it the *Luzeiro* (Portuguese for "Light Bearer"), stocked it with as much quinine, Epsom salts, salves and bandages as he could buy or scrounge —and set out with Jessie.

Leo knew less about navigation than he did about doctoring, and it took some harrowing experiences to accustom him to the Amazon's treacherous currents and moods. Today old river hands testify, "Nobody knows the Amazon better."

The moods of the Indians were equally difficult. Most of the tribes, fleeing the white man's advance, had settled along the headwaters of the Amazon's tributaries. Living a primeval existence, many fiercely resisted with blow guns and poisoned arrows the encroachments of strangers.

At sight of the *Luzeiro* in the Andira River the Indians of the Maués tribe fled in terror; they had never seen a "canoe" like this. Halliwell brought out his victrola and put on a band record. Presently the Indians crept out of the woods, crowded around the instrument, chattering among themselves. They were just as amazed by the miraculously quick effects of quinine on malaria fever then raging in the village.

The Halliwells soon learned to begin their annual odyssey upriver early in February, after the river had begun its mighty rise (in some places as high as 60 feet). It reaches full flood stage in May and June and that season supplies the most water for easy access to the people; it also creates the greatest needs. Floodtime is inevitably tragedy-time for Amazon dwellers; the forest is inundated and homes are washed away. On each voyage, Halliwell told the people the approximate time of his return, asked them to hang out a white cloth to signal their need. Soon every mile of his journey was lined with fluttering cloths. For three consecutive years, Mrs. Halliwell delivered the babies of the wife of the mayor of a certain town. How did the blessed events happen to coincide with the *Luzeiro's* visits? "I planned it that way," said the wife.

Dangerous as was the constant threat from jungle beasts and reptiles, the swarms of flying and crawling things produced even more misery and death. An unbelievable variety of insects—flies, bugs, bees, ants, wasps, ticks, chiggers—assailed the people day and night.

The most serious menace to health in the Amazon was malaria. At every stop Halliwell was greeted by listless, half-alive people aflame with fever.

The throb of the *Luzeiro's* motors became a song of hope up and down the Amazon and its maze of waterways. Soon he was treating as many as 300 malaria patients a day, distributing up to 50,000 quinine tablets a year.

At one place the Halliwells were flagged by a man in a canoe who led them to a home that was one large room with a center pole supporting the thatched roof. From the pole to the side walls, like spokes in a wheel, were stretched 22 hammocks. In each lay a victim burning with high fever. By the time Leo had treated them, word had spread and canoes by the score were arriving. Some bore sick, others carried messengers begging him to come to relatives or friends. In one home he found a 10-year-old girl, whose entire family had been taken by the fever. She had tried to bury her mother, father and older brother, but was too weak from fever to dig deep graves. When Halliwell arrived, dogs had unearthed the bodies and were dragging portions about the yard.

In the beginning he used injections of quinine and methy-line blue, then counted out enough quinine capsules to leave with the patients for follow-up. Later, when such products as atabrine, cloroquin and camouquin became available, he used these in the same immense quantities.

When leaving medicines with the people, Halliwell learned to make crystal clear his instructions for their use. Once he returned after three days to be told by the wife of a patient that her husband had taken all 67 grains of quinine in one gulp. Halliwell inquired anxiously, "Did he die?" The woman replied, "Oh, no. His ears rang a little, but it cured him. He's out in the field working!"

Another time his instructions went awry was when he left some medicine for a small boy. "How will I know when to give the doses?" asked the mother. "We have no clock." Halliwell replied, "You have a rooster? When he crows give him a dose." When he dropped by days later to inquire about the boy, the woman reported, "My boy's fine now—but the rooster died!"

Halliwell himself had been 15 years in the Amazon before he got malaria. In a river town he had stopped off to help a Catholic priest for two days, sweatily getting his brother Christian's power plant in order. When he came back to the boat, he was too tired to close the screens. The resulting malaria kept him inactive for weeks. But on the whole, using proper precautions and taking his own medicine, he and his wife maintained exuberant health amid rampant sickness of all kinds.

At first the Halliwells had to purchase medicines from their slender mission resources, then enlist young people of the Belém church to put them in capsules and bottles. In later years their medicine chest was kept supplied by doctors and pharmaceutical houses in the United States, and by the public health departments of the states of Pará and Amazonas. During World War II, when quinine was almost unobtainable, an American wholesale drug dealer in Argentina called Halliwell to his office. He unlocked a large depository, pointed to stacked piles of quinine and said, "Look closely." On every wrapper Halliwell's name was written. "That's our entire stock," he said. "But I want you to have it!"

Governors of several Brazilian states soon were making generous personal contributions to Halliwell. One said, "No one is doing so much for my people. Please let me help."

Second only to malaria as a debilitator of the people, Halliwell early discovered, was the hookworm. Fully 90 per cent of the river dwellers had worms. A safe rule of thumb was, "When in diagnostic doubt, give a dose of worm medicine."

In the early years, the *Luzeiro* carried huge stores of Epsom salts and castor oil. The people took these remedies without question, often begged for more—whatever their trouble. Typical was the old man who came one day to the boat deck where Halliwell was busy injecting for malaria. The old man had no fever, but his appearance shouted hookworms. Halliwell gave him a dose of salts, promising, "This will make you 10 years younger." On the next trip, he found the old man at the head of the settlement's waiting line, spry and grinning. He wanted another dose. "I'd like to lose another 10 years!" he said.

Skin troubles abounded. In Amazonia, the least abrasion provides entry for blood-lapping vampire bats, larvae-hatching blowflies and screwworms that cause huge abscesses, yaws, ulcers. In one typical year, Halliwell used more than 1000 injections of penicillin for yaws.

Eye diseases, too, took their toll. On an island in the lower Amazon he found a family of 12, all nearly blind with trachoma. He left them a bottle of sulphathiozole tablets to stave off the disease's progress, advised them to take the next steamer to the city to consult a good eye doctor. Four months later he stopped at the island to check, found that all had completely recovered—without going to the city for treatment.

As a rule, the Halliwells avoided treating complicated diseases, making arrangements to send severe cases to the nearest town. But jungle life is full of emergencies. One day while passing down a river, they heard screams. An alligator had seized a girl while she was washing clothes in the river. Her brother hammered the beast over the head until it let go, but the girl was horribly mangled. Halliwell bandaged her wounds and saved her life. Today the girl is an Adventist worker.

Another time, he had to treat a man who had just lost a leg while asleep in a canoe. In turning over in his sleep, the man stuck his foot out over the edge, and the 'gator had snapped off his leg at the knee. Later killed, the reptile measured over 20 feet long.

Halliwell believed that religious faith played an important part in many of his more unorthodox healings. There was, for example, the young man convert in a tiny village upriver. His face horribly disfigured by leprosy, his body covered with large sores, he had been forbidden by the other villagers to leave his house. Yet he had a burning zeal to be a Christian evangelist. Halliwell obtained some chaulmoogra oil, gave him a few treatments, then left a quantity with careful instructions as to its injection.

A year later, he returned to discover the boy had not only made big improvement but had converted nine other persons—having induced his sister to invite neighbors into an adjoining room so that he could stand at his door to preach to them. After hundreds of injections, mostly self-administered, the youth finally recovered completely, has 23 certificates from public health authorities attesting to his cure, is now devoting his life to helping other lepers along the river.

The Halliwells never made any charge for their services. However, in gratitude, the river people often brought little gifts, shyly depositing them on the *Luzeiro's* deck—a squash, an egg, pieces of deer meat, small bunches of bananas.

Only rarely did Halliwell meet opposition from the medical profession and never from Brazilian doctors. Despite his lack of a medical degree, his aid and counsel were frequently sought by medical societies.

Some Indians, however, did oppose him. The chief of the Maués, Caetano, was willing to assign land for a school which Halliwell started with the help of a Brazilian teacher, but he disdained gringo medicine and religion for himself. Then a smallpox epidemic ravaged the village. Caetano allowed Halliwell to vaccinate every survivor—except himself. He refused to let the white man "puncture my arm." On the Halliwells' next visit, months later, they found the old chief in his hut, covered with smallpox. He gasped through parched lips, "I wrong. When disease come, I only man to get it. Please puncture me now."

In 1955 Caetano accepted Christianity, quickly became

a help in spreading it among other tribes. Today the school and church at the Maués village are thriving—as are many others started in Amazonia by the Halliwells.

Halliwell became the Indians' trusted friend. A few years ago, when a promoter of rosewood distilling moved up the Andira to establish a plant in their territory, five Maués chiefs assembled the tribes, prepared 2000 poisoned arrows to kill him and all his workers. They were on the point of attack when Halliwell came up the river. To the chiefs he said, "You have right on your side. But your action will only bring more trouble. Go instead to the authorities at Manaus." The chiefs nodded gravely, "White medicine man's counsel is good. We do." And the matter was settled without bloodshed.

In order to reach still more people Leo equipped the *Luzeiro* with a generator that would provide power and illumination for a sound projector. Using colored slides and films with a Portuguese sound track, the Halliwells held classes regularly in river-bank clearings. Such modern gadgets at first startled then delighted the people. One woman, upon hearing a soprano tuned in from New York on Halliwell's short-wave radio, demanded, "What that?" When told it was "a woman thousands of miles away singing to us," she exclaimed, wide-eyed, "*Mae de Deus,* what a pair of lungs!"

Immense crowds came to look and listen, many people paddling in canoes for hours to reach the jungle classroom, where they learned, among other things, about nutrition and were encouraged to plant gardens to supplement their vitamin-poor diet.

One day Halliwell noted several children with bleeding

gums—scurvy. Near their hut were lime trees; he picked some of the limes, juiced them in tea, wheedled the mother into promising to give it to her children regularly. Returning weeks later, he found the children's gums healed and a local fad started for "lime tea."

From an American friend in Manaus, Jessie collected choice grapefruit seeds and distributed them. Today, all along the river grapefruit trees abound and vitamin C deficiency has notably decreased. Along the Amazon, too, there are healthy babies, many of them named "Jessie" and "Leo."

When the Halliwells first came, the infant mortality rate in the Amazon Valley was 64 per cent. This has been impressively reduced in areas they regularly visited, in one region dropping as low as 10 per cent.

Among the Indians, Mrs. Halliwell learned, it was customary for the wife to have her baby alone in the forest, being considered unclean. She would take it to a stream to wash it, then go back to work—while her husband would put a towel over his head, lie down in his hammock for three days, groaning with the pangs of childbirth and coming parenthood. Indignant, she shamed such spouses into more responsibility and helpfulness. In some villages, as the result of her crusade, the custom is now extinct.

The Halliwells also did much to revise hymeneal habits. Among Brazilian nationals especially, they found matrimony a free and easy affair. When smitten with the mating impulse, a man and woman just moved in together—without benefit of ceremony. There being no divorce law in Brazil, a couple fed up with each other simply separated and sought more congenial partners.

Tests for Indian grooms were more stringent. For him the

tribe would prepare a pair of straw gloves, inserting in each a hive of poisonous insects capable of swelling a man's arms to twice their size. Around his knees a string of small bells would record any slightest quaking when the insects went to work. Before him stood his intended bride, ready to reject him at the bells' first tinkle. Survival of the test meant the pair were duly wed—and could hang up the gloves in their home as their marriage certificate.

Since Brazilian law does not recognize a religious ceremony alone as legal, and since the Amazon areas were exceedingly shy of qualified officials, Halliwell spent years arguing about "enforced immorality," finally talked the state of Amazonas into supplying a "marrying judge" for each section.

The Halliwells made Christian as well as civil marriage one of the first requirements of converts. Soon he was marrying people who had lived together for as long as 40 years. On his later trips he conducted many weddings, among them one for a couple whose oldest son, with a family of his own, was best man. The *Luzeiro*, besides being a home for the Halliwells, a church for the churchless, a hospital, clinic and ambulance, was often a gaily decorated wedding chapel.

Leo Halliwell met nautical mishaps with ingenuity. He had to: there were no machine shops between Belém and Manaus, a 1000-mile stretch. His only drydock was the shore. When something went wrong, he would pull his vessel as close in as possible, wait for the tide to go down. When the water receded, the *Luzeiro* settled on dry land and he had several hours to work before the incoming tide set him afloat again.

An ever-present danger was from logs floating just beneath the surface. One morning, while crossing the river at a point several miles wide and 300 feet deep, there was a sickening crash and water began to pour in from a large hole in the hull. Leo grabbed up a long strip of canvas, called to Jessie, and the two passed a loop under the hull and worked it over the hole, where the water pressure held it in place until he could bail out the water and fasten a board over the stove-in spot.

A sense of God's protecting hand gave him confidence, made him fearless. One day several years ago, the *Luzeiro* suddenly burst into flames. A careless boat boy had spilled gasoline when filling the stove. Leo grabbed a woolen blanket, rushed into the flaming galley, threw the blanket over the stove, heaved both overboard. The fire burned the spilled fuel on the floor without catching the wood—"as if put out by the hand of the Lord." That night, before they went to sleep, Jessie opened the Bible and read aloud: "When thou passest through the waters, I will be with thee. When thou walkest through the fire, thou shalt not be burned, neither shall the flame kindle upon thee."

A flood-time hazard to reaching people who live along smaller streams and on shores of backed-up lakes are floating grass islands. Looking like great pastures adrift, these clog channel entrances, require hours of work to pole them aside.

An incident shortly after starting his Amazon work taught Leo never to pass up a place where he was expected, if it were humanly possible to reach it. A convert named Ribeiro had settled on a lake, separated from the river by a five-mile channel, where dwelt some 60 families. He sent Halliwell word that two weeks of meetings and medicines might Christianize the whole village.

Arriving at the channel, Leo found it blocked, decided

to pass on and make the visit next year. But next year, a tearful Ribeiro met him at the channel's now clear mouth. "It's too late," he cried. "The fever came and took them all. I alone am left!"

Halliwell went up the channel to the lake, saw the abandoned homes whose emptiness seemed to accuse him, sorrowed for months that he had let "the river snatch these souls from us."

At such times the river seemed an enemy, dark and threatening—an enemy not to be surrendered to under any circumstances. But such moods were rare. The Halliwells, for all its raw savagery, loved the Amazon—even as they loved its people. At evening, exhausted and weary, they would turn into some quiet *igarape,* anchor beside a bank bordering jungle a thousand miles deep—and revel in their lot.

During the day the jungle may possess a silence like deafness. But when night comes down—swiftly, without twilight—it breaks into sounds like no other on earth. These, to the Halliwells, were the sounds of home. Beloved, serene, secure. To preserve them, he made a tape recording some years ago. And when away from the river on furlough or business trips to far cities, he would close his hotel door to the raucous revels of radio and television, uncover his recorder, put the tape on, and contentedly go to sleep to Amazon night sounds—the deep croak of frogs and the shrill chatter of cicadas, the alligator grunts and monkey howls, the stealthy sound of animals moving through the brush only yards away, the gentle slap of the river against the boat.

Stimulated by the example of Leo and Jessie Halliwell, other missionaries have come to the Amazon and volunteered

for launch duty. Today a fleet of eight carbon copies of the
Luzeiro are plying the river and its tributaries; during a
recent year 27,000 major medical cases were treated. Proving
Leo's thesis that "medical work is the right arm of the Gospel," there are today along the Amazon 22 Adventist
churches with some 3000 baptized members and 56 Sabbath
Schools and 15 elementary schools teaching 1000 youngsters. In the vast territory once tilled only by himself and
Jessie, his church today has 15 ministers, a score of teachers
and doctors.

The Halliwells' long battle against the ravages of malaria
has also borne fruit. Today, through SESP (*Serviço Es-
pecial de Saúde Pública*), a mutual aid program of public
health jointly sponsored by the United States and Brazil,
a huge malaria control program is under way. An American
doctor working with SESP told me, "If it hadn't been for
the Halliwells, it is not likely that this or any other agency
would have been set up. They proved what could be done."

Only recently Halliwell saw a long dream come true.
In 1942, completely on faith and without funds, he opened a
tiny clinic in Belém and called a Brazilian doctor to run it.
Now that clinic has metamorphosed into a fully equipped
40-bed hospital.

One day in 1956, Leo Halliwell got word that he was
needed in Rio de Janeiro to supervise the work of all Adventist medical launches throughout South America.
Obliquely Halliwell put the matter to Jessie. Wasn't it getting crowded on the Amazon, with so many launches and all
these workers and churches? Besides, now that they were
along in years, wouldn't the climate be a little easier in some
place like, say, Rio de Janeiro?

Jessie smiled knowingly. "When do we leave, Leo?"

In July they turned the *Luzeiro* over to another missionary, and headed south. Thus, at 65, when most people are ready to retire, the Halliwells were starting all over again.

"Leo," said a colleague seeing them off, "is still looking for latitude!"

X

"The Gospel of the Plow"

On an April evening in 1919, a husky young teacher from Washington State was jolted out of a deep sleep by the sound of jungle drums and weird chanting. Only that day Emory Alvord, with his bride, had arrived at this remote spot in Southern Rhodesia to begin work. He sat bolt upright, listening, then rushed outside. He came upon a sight that shook him to his shoestrings.

Over an acre of stumpy, neglected farmland a milling crowd of African men and women, led by whirling witchdoctors, were prancing and shrieking appeals to the gods of the soil. When they fell exhausted, black arms gathered them in, revived them with gourds of potent native beer, and what seemed like a wild orgy went on.

Alvord watched. So this was native agriculture. He had been told what to expect. On the long, hazardous journey to his station—7000 miles by ship, six days and 1628 miles by train into the interior, and 14 days and 174 miles by donkey-wagon to Mt. Silinda Mission—old Africa hands had warned him that vigor was something the African farmer had little of; voodoo was his tool.

Now, through the eerie firelight and the clouds of dust, Emory Alvord thought he saw these people as they really were. Lazy? No lazy man would expend such energy.

194

Superstitious? Perhaps, but was not superstition itself a sort of faith? Redirect that energy and faith, and . . .

Striding back to his mission station in the morning's chill dawn, he mapped out a program which he dubbed "The Gospel of the Plow." He was Africa's first agricultural missionary.

Today, Emory Alvord's faith in the natives ("Bantu") of Rhodesia has been spectacularly justified. Under his tutelage they have literally changed the face of their country. Vast numbers of them enjoy a sense of prosperity and community well-being unknown in other regions of the Dark Continent.

The pioneering instinct runs strong in Alvord blood. The family settled in Connecticut in 1632. Emory's great-grandfather went to Utah in 1847. His grandfather ran mule trains through the new West, and was found murdered beside his campfire. His father fought in the Philippines and did construction work there and in Alaska.

Emory himself chose farming for a career, worked his way through Idaho State Normal and Washington State College. At both schools he captained the football squad.

While washing windows in the gymnasium to help pay his way through Idaho Normal, he lost his balance and fell three stories, smashing his foot so badly that doctors said he was through as an athlete. But when football practice started, five months later, Alvord reported—on crutches. Exertions on the gridiron caused excruciating pain for weeks, but they restored the crippled foot to partial use, though he was left with a limp for four years. Even this had its points: the limp gave him what sports writers called a "plunging gallop," making him a tough man to tackle. Upon graduation he received tempting offers to make football his career. He chose instead to teach agriculture at Washington State.

Then in 1918 he began to look for a frontier for himself. Gregarious, he wanted a frontier that was humanitarian. He volunteered for life service as an agricultural missionary. Asked why, he said, "The human race must stand together. The strong and qualified must help the weak. It is my aim to teach Christianity through the unexcelled medium of agriculture, full as it is of reverential objects which remind us hourly of God and life."

The missionary idea of saving souls by saving soil was comparatively new. He was assigned to Southern Rhodesia, a self-governing British colony about the size of California, deep in the center of Africa's southern tip. Sometimes said to be the ancient site of King Solomon's mines, the land had been fought over for centuries by Arabs, Portuguese and others. Then, decades ago, the gold-seekers had departed and the whole region sank into somnolence until Cecil Rhodes and his British South Africa Company grabbed it for king and country.

The mission at Mt. Silinda, begun in the early 1890's on 30,000 acres granted by Rhodes, majored in Christian education and handcraft. Agriculture, around which the whole of native life revolved, was not stressed. When mission associates lamented that making converts was easy but keeping them faithful was impossible when they returned to their homes, Alvord asked: "What else can you expect? You can't build a good society, let alone the Kingdom of God, on eroding soil and eroding people!"

He promptly laid out six demonstration plots. At the first

harvest season he invited the Bantu from miles around to see the maize plants 12 feet high bearing 12-inch cobs—quite a contrast with the native plants two or three feet tall, with cobs no bigger than a man's thumb.

Triumphantly, Alvord expounded the merits of proper tillage. His bubbling spirits simmered down a bit when he asked them if they understood, and they shouted, "Yes, yes. You great witch-doctor!" Even the mission pupils who had cultivated the plots under his direction were convinced he had gone out during the night and sprinkled magic medicine.

He knew then that he must persuade the Bantu to put his methods to work on their own plots, where all could see that there was nothing supernatural. The Alvord formula was simple: clear the land properly, water it, fertilize it with kraal manure now being wasted, rotate the crops.

To the pitiable farmers on their pitifully worn-out plots, he would say, "What is this land you have? It's a trust for your children and your children's children. God has loaned it to you to use, not destroy. He sends the rain and warmth of the sun. All He expects of you is that you love your land, nourish it, co-operate with it. God wants you and your families to have the good things of life; He's given you the raw materials to make a good life. He wants you to work with Him."

He moved among the people as a fellow-worker of the soil, eager to help. In casual conversations he painted such a beguiling picture that more and more natives volunteered their land for his experiments. They found that plots properly tilled would yield ten times as much as before. Even the worst land blossomed under proper tillage. When in 1922 most Bantu crops failed completely, Alvord's students and demonstrators produced good yields.

The witch-doctors and other bush-league dervishes, sensing ruinous competition, heckled him at the demonstrations, shouting to the people that the gods of the soil would visit dire punishment on any African dabbling in the white man's sorcery.

Word of his success with the natives reached government officials at Salisbury. They promptly invited him to take a job as government agriculturist. In 1926 he accepted, seeing a chance to spread his Gospel of the Plow far beyond the mission's confines. His appointment was vigorously opposed by some elements who resented a missionary, especially an American, in any job of importance in a British colony. Many officials too had a dim view of doing anything at all for natives, stuffily insisting that a government agriculturist's job was to aid European farmers. He finally got himself transferred to the Department of Native Affairs so there would be no question about whom he was hired to help.

During his first year as government agriculturist Alvord stepped up acreage production sixfold on demonstration plots. His huge bulk packed behind the wheel of his small British car became a familiar sight everywhere in the native reserves. Sometimes he walked for miles through jungle or open veldt to inspect demonstration plots too remote to reach by car. Natives came to expect this white-thatched man on his lonely safari, a bag of improved seed over his shoulder. On Sundays he took his place in the choir of their little churches, looking like a great white bear among dark cubs.

The next few years Emory Alvord seemed to be every-

where at once—organizing courses in missionary and government schools, setting up more and more demonstration plots
and experimental stations, arranging gala farm shows, introducing more diversified products, making soil surveys,
directing the installation of a vast irrigation system, laying
out model villages. By 1949 a total of 72,849 demonstration
plots had been set up; on them the average yield was seven
times what it was on adjacent fields.

Knowing the Bantu's fondness for personal decoration as
well as community prestige, Alvord developed an ornate
enamel badge, richly scrolled with "Master Farmer," and
awarded it to those whose plots were consistently superior.
In some cases, there being no place to pin it, the badge was
worn on a string around the neck; others improvised head-
bands to properly display it, while one devised a way to
dangle it from his left ear. Eventually there were some
1200 "Master Farmers" throughout Rhodesia.

By 1950, the art of scientific farming, now a required subject in all schools for natives, was being taught to 170,000
pupils yearly. Almost half of all Bantu farmers were doing
their work under the guidance of trained government demonstrators drawn from their own ranks. Eleven million acres
had been centralized into arable and grazing lands, and the
best methods of crop rotation, irrigation and soil conserva-
tion had been applied to hundreds of thousands of acres.
Seven large breeding stations were steadily improving
cattle strains.

To oversee this skyrocketing program of native development, initiated and personally directed by Emory Alvord,
the government of Southern Rhodesia maintained a staff
of 70 Europeans and 436 native experts in its Department of

Native Agriculture. In the beginning, Alvord was the whole department. His work at first cost the government little; he taught the Bantu how to carry the expense of their own improvement, instilled in them a pride in doing so.

A village headman told him one day of the sickness that periodically swept the village. Alvord led the headman over to one of the "pole and dagga" huts, showed him how such construction made for dampness, draftiness, the increase of vermin. Then he drew a sketch of a thatched brick house. "Wouldn't you like one like that?" he asked. Next day he and the headman began work; the house became a show-place for miles around.

Next he started teaching a group of young men in each village the art of brickmaking, stonework, roof construction. Pupils completing the course were given a Builder's Certificate; they in turn became contractors and teachers of others. Today more than 58 per cent of Rhodesia's native population live in improved houses designed by Alvord and built by the natives themselves. Moreover, 1500 schools and churches have also been built.

Alvord introduced corn from Iowa to replace the Kaffir variety, and started the natives at raising cotton. Today there are some 12,000 native cotton-growers, and production has reached an estimated five million pounds of seed cotton for 1950. Government-sponsored and native-operated ginning mills produce yarn. Thousands of African natives are now clothed in cotton goods produced by themselves.

In 1935, during a severe famine, he was seized with the importance of wide-scale irrigation. With no funds, but plenty of official resistance, he decided to dramatize irrigation's worth. At Nyanyadzi, an area particularly hard hit, all able-bodied men were away working for Europeans to get money to buy food. Loaded down with picks and shovels, Alvord came to Nyanyadzi with a flourish, surveyed and pegged the canals, persuaded 26 women and three old men to help him dig, and eventually reaped an average of 48 bushels of grain per acre from land where not more than five had ever been harvested before. When the husbands returned they found their families fat and flourishing and with more food than they could possibly buy with the money the men brought back.

The demonstration impressed the government too. Funds became available for more irrigation. Two years later, Alvord and a host of willing volunteers together dug his biggest canal in the same Nyanyadzi River district—4½ miles long, 10 feet wide, three feet deep. No gang boss, he seized a shovel himself and helped dig, setting a pace for the workers.

The project consumed six months. At its official opening, a feast day for the entire region, thousands of African natives went wild with excitement as the headgates lifted and the wave of water plunged into the canal. Men, women and children, yelling and singing hymns, swarmed in, splashing the muddy water on each other and lapping it up in their mouths. To Alvord the mothers explained: "Oh, *N'kosimuchena* (king with the white hair), we want to tell our children when we grow old that we and they drank some of the first water of life that came to bless our land!"

All this had to be done over bitter opposition. European farmers felt Alvord's interest in Africans was an offense to white dignity and a threat to the stability of the status quo. He got threatening letters—"You ought to be shot." Corn, they protested, was a white man's crop. Cotton-growing by the natives was upsetting the whole economy. And there were government officials who took the same view and were obstructionists. Alvord went blithely ahead.

With improved farming methods and improved homes came the need for better tools and better furnishings to go with them. Alvord discussed with his Bantu friends the special kind of cart they needed, with their help drew a design, took to the government officials his idea for a small plant. The plant was established, Alvord schooled 18 young Bantu in cart-making, and within three years hundreds of low-cost substantial carts were rolling across the farms and veldts of Rhodesia.

When resentful white settlers used Alvord's American citizenship as an excuse for opposing his program, he applied for citizenship in Rhodesia. In 1937 he was awarded the King's Coronation Medal, and later was made an Officer of the Civil Division of the Order of the British Empire.

Upon his retirement in 1950 Alvord sat through the laudatory speeches, obviously ill at ease. But when a wizened little old Bantu chief stood up and said, "Cecil Rhodes founded this country but Emory Alvord has founded a people!"— Alvord wept unashamedly.

The retirement business over, his first act was to take his wife to see Victoria Falls; they had been in Rhodesia 31 years, yet "just somehow never had found time" to visit the famed tourist attraction. That done, they came back to America for six months—and traveled all over the States by bus, picking up fresh ideas for transplantation to Rhodesia.

Just before he and Mrs. Alvord sailed back to Mt. Silinda Mission in 1951, "to serve out the lifetime we originally pledged," Alvord said: "I believe more firmly than ever in the infinite potential in people—any people, all people. But their improvement must come always from within themselves. I have no faith in handouts of any kind, economic or spiritual. Abraham Lincoln once said, 'You cannot help men permanently by doing for them what they could and should do for themselves.' We need to inscribe that statement large across every plan we make these days—and we're making some big ones—for aiding the earth's backward peoples."

XI

Servant of the Poor

On a February morning in 1946 a little man in baggy trousers and a borrowed frock coat strode briskly into the Imperial palace at Tokyo. His wife had pinned up the coat, for it was several sizes too large; but it kept slipping and from time to time he had to hitch it up onto his shoulders.

Emperor Hirohito, struggling to orient himself to his suddenly acquired status of humanity, had invited this man of the slums to "lecture" him on the finer points of democracy, tell him how he, too, might become a man of the people.

The lecture, slated for a half hour, lasted three times as long. The emperor listened intently. Finally the speaker drew out a battered Bible and read: " 'Whosoever will be great among you . . . shall be servant of all.' A ruler's sovereignty, Your Majesty, is in the hearts of his people. Only by service to others can a man, or a nation, be god-like."

Thus did Hirohito, "Son of Heaven," come face to face for the first time with Toyohiko Kagawa, son of a philandering politician and a concubine.

The advice given his emperor that day was, in essence, the credo Kagawa has been living and preaching for nearly 50

204

Leo Halliwell of Brazil at the wheel of his launch of mercy, the *Luzeiro* (Portuguese for "light-bearer"). (Chapter IX)

A familiar sight on the Amazon's 1000-mile stretch from Belém to Manaus, the Halliwells' aquatic clinic brings medicines—and the Gospel—to tens of thousands of river-dwellers who have no other doctor or minister.

Trevor Huddleston, Anglican priest whose daring fight for the rights of Africans in Johannesburg's Negro slums won him government hatred and world admiration, making one of his stirring pleas against "apartheid" in the Union of South Africa. (Chapter VIII)

Toyohiko Kagawa, renowned Japanese reformer and product of Christian missions, with children of his Matsuzawa Church in Tokyo. (Chapter XI)

years, during a career as fabulous as that of Francis of Assisi, as turbulent as that of St. Paul.

Japan's most prolific author, founder of the empire's co-operative movement, organizer and director of trade unions, tireless proponent of farm reform, Kagawa has done a job which has affected the face of Japan's social order in many ways. More important, he has been chiefly responsible for keeping that face from adopting the likeness of Karl Marx.

As early as 1921 he became a target for the Kremlin's attacks, and he has remained so to this day. "Communism's only power is to diagnose some of the pathology of disordered society," says Kagawa. "It has no cure. It creates only an infantile paralysis of the social order."

Born out of wedlock, Kagawa was legally adopted by his father at the age of five and packed off to the untender care of the philanderer's neglected wife and her indignant mother. These two embittered women took turns beating the boy. Only when he was sent away to school at Tokushima did he learn that there was love and tenderness in the world. For here he met two American missionary teachers, Dr. Harry W. Myers and Dr. Charles A. Logan.

Observing the youngster's tortured loneliness, they took him into their hearts and homes. They taught him to know that all men are created by a God of love, and that any person devoting himself to serving his fellow men can work tremendous changes for good. They put into his hands a Book that revealed the character of the Christian God. It was while he was memorizing the Sermon on the Mount that there was born in Kagawa the passion which became the rudder of his life: to lift the downtrodden, love the loveless, serve the oppressed.

When Toyohiko's family heard he had been baptized in the Christian faith, he was promptly disinherited. With a feeling of relief and almost gay abandon, he plunged furiously into studying for the Christian ministry. He overdid it, and in his second year at Tokyo's Presbyterian College he was struck down by tuberculosis.

His friends got up a purse and sent him to the seashore for a year. Sure that he was going to die, he devoted himself to writing the first draft of a serious novel—on assorted scraps of paper and the backs of can labels. When he had bundled up this decrepit manuscript he gave himself over to racking hemorrhages.

But suddenly he decided that heaven would have to wait. With superhuman effort he roused himself and somehow got to Tokyo. Later he enrolled, sick as he was, in the Kobe Theological Seminary.

While studying there, Kagawa found that the seminarians' endless concern for technicalities of creed and doctrine palled on him. Christian ethics to him meant Christian action. Impatiently he would point to the parable of the Good Samaritan and demand: "What is there to discuss? Isn't this plain enough?" And off he would go to Kobe's infamous Shinkawa slums, whose tragedies were as poignant to him as anything on the Jericho road.

Shinkawa was the last word in slums. Into its filthy alleys and verminous shacks were sardined 11,000 persons, a miserable motley of the poor and unemployed, liberally sprinkled with beggars, gamblers, thieves, pimps, and prostitutes. Here was a laboratory for testing the validity of the Sermon on the Mount. If it would work here, it would work anywhere.

On Christmas eve, 1909, Kagawa carted his few possessions from the seminary to Shinkawa's only vacancy, a six-by-six-foot hut which was available only because it was reputedly haunted. Here he was to live and work for 15 years. Here he was to dream his dreams and bring them to life, here develop the ideas and ideals which made him world famous, here write most of his more than 100 books.

His neighbors were chary at first. Then, as it became plain that he wanted nothing but a chance to serve them, they moved in with him—the sick, the poverty-stricken, the deranged. When his "guests" ate up his monthly seminary scholarship of $5.50, he became a chimney sweep and provided another $5 a month. When that was gone he watered down his rice gruel to make it go around.

To occasional visitors he would proudly display his parish, calling it "my little kingdom of the slums." When they called him a fool, he amended it to "Christ's fool" and gloried in the appellation.

Beggars of the baser sort caught on quickly to the potentials of such a Christian in their midst. One asked for Kagawa's shirt, and when he got it demanded also his coat and pants—quoting Scripture to back his expectations. Kagawa gave them all. Whereupon a reformed prostitute came to his aid with a woman's kimono, which he wore about the streets for days, its flaming red lining arousing raucous merriment.

Gamblers and ruffians demanded money of him, and when he had no more to give they assaulted him with stones and daggers, broke the windows of his hut. One knocked out four of his front teeth.

Kagawa never struck back. He eschewed violence, for

whatever cause. Besides, beneath their filth and roughness he saw these miserable ones not as degenerates but as human souls who would respond to Christian love if given a chance.

In time they did, flocking to him with their problems, bringing their children to his Sunday school held in a vacant lot, fighting off his attackers, contributing their mites so that he could help others.

One day a publisher, visiting Shinkawa in search of copy, called during Kagawa's absence. Poking around the hut he found the bundle of scrap paper on which Kagawa had written his novel while waiting to die. When Kagawa returned he found a check for advance royalties. *"Across the Death Line,"* first run as a magazine serial and later issued in book form, was an instantaneous best seller; some 250,000 copies were sold in an incredibly short time.

With his first royalties Kagawa added a room to his hut to serve as dispensary and hospital. To this day he uses his income—now some $50,000 a year—to further his Christian projects, keeping only enough for frugal living.

Amazed that people would buy his writings, Kagawa now drove himself relentlessly. Here was a way to tell the world about the slums and fight for the correction of their evils! But he had no place to work. So, waiting until his "guests" were asleep, he would sit on the floor among them and write till dawn.

Soon book after book had thrust him and his flaming ideas into the Japanese consciousness. When in 1924 his government moved to wipe out the slums in Japan's six largest cities, his writings were given the main credit.

The evolution of Kagawa from simple servant of the poor

into social reformer began in 1914 when his friends staked him to two years of study at Princeton Theological Seminary. Convinced that poverty made slums, and that the inequities dealt the laborer made poverty, he entered the labor movement.

It was a critical time. Japan's switch from feudalism to the machine age had begun. But the shiny new machines were installed in miserable sweatshops without light or air, and the laborers worked long hours at pittance pay. Sporadic efforts had been made to organize labor, but any union was illegal and all agitators were promptly jailed.

Kagawa began writing on the evils of worker exploitation and openly proclaimed, "Laborers are personalities, not goods to be bought and sold. They must be given the right to organize."

It was for this right, not for increased wages and shorter hours, that in 1921 Kobe's thousands of dockyard workers went on strike. Kagawa had opposed the strike, pleading for peaceful negotiation. But when they surged up his alley crying, "Lead us, Kagawa!" he accepted the challenge, organized them into Japan's first full-fledged labor union.

The police seized him, tearing his clothes and beating him with a saber, and dragged him off to jail. It was only after his release, 13 days later, that he learned how effectively the assiduous Communists had spread word among the strikers that his insistence on nonviolence stamped him as an idealistic fool—or the employers' tool. The only way to break down a capitalist was to break up his machines. Secret plans had been laid for a march of destruction on the shipyards.

The next day some 35,000 men, armed with bricks and crowbars, came surging down the road toward the largest yard. There were no guards to stop them—and only one obstacle. Standing on a narrow bridge over which they had to pass was a solitary figure, blocking their way. The mob flowed up to the bridge, came to an abashed halt. The figure did not speak; he simply stood there, praying silently. It was Kagawa. The men, ashamed, turned and went away.

In 1925, largely because of his influence, the law forbidding unions was repealed.

Meanwhile the sad condition of Japanese farmers was making fertile soil for Communists. Kagawa proceeded to write the "farm problem" into his novels, lectured about it up and down the land.

When in 1921 a deputation of farmers came to his hut to invite his counsel, he formed them at once into the nucleus of an agrarian reform movement. In a matter of days he had started a new magazine, *The Soil and Freedom*. And in a few months he had sparked an All-Japan Peasants' conference, at which was launched the Japan Peasants' union.

Central in this peasant awakening was Kagawa's fathering of producers' co-operatives. The movement spread like a brush fire, the flight from the land was arrested, and rural living took on new dignity as well as some prosperity. By 1935 virtually all of Japan's 5,500,000 farmers were members of co-ops, which included not only wholesaler and consumer groups but those providing medical services, credit, rural housing, crop insurance.

The long war he waged against the militarists probably brought him into more official disfavor than his social reforms. In 1928 he boldly founded the National Anti-War League of Japan, declaring flatly against the burgeoning schemes of the war lords, and organizing an educational campaign in behalf of peace. This league at one time numbered tens of thousands of members. But when the military clique launched the "China incident," many supporters fell by the wayside.

Not Kagawa. He flew to China and there, in the ruins of a Shanghai church, tearfully apologized for the wrongs his countrymen had done and pleaded for Chinese forgiveness for himself and his nation. For this the militarists clapped him into prison when he returned.

As the threat of war with America increased, Kagawa frantically stepped up his peace efforts and was in and out of jail repeatedly. The news from Pearl Harbor broke his heart, and the years 1941–45 were the bleakest and most tragic of his life.

His great network of co-ops, with their millions of members, were nationalized and regimented; his labor unions were abolished; his rural rehabilitation projects were jettisoned. Many of the institutions he had founded—settlements, orphanages, Christian service centers, chapels—were destroyed in bombing raids. The militarists persuaded him, "in humanity's name," to broadcast protests against American obliteration bombing. They made recordings of his broadcasts, adroitly tacked on inflammatory propaganda, and beamed them to America, which he had visited often and where he had many admirers.

Following his doctored broadcasts he was attacked in the Western press as a warmonger. Most of the jibes were inspired by a searing attack made on him in the Pacific edition of *Stars and Stripes*. Based on an interview shortly after the war, the story carried the headline: "Under Christian Guise This Jap Fostered War!"

Widely quoted in America, the broadside shook church-men's faith in Kagawa. Its echoes are still being heard. The attack falls into better perspective when one learns that both the columnist who wrote the story and his manag-ing editor were removed from their posts a few weeks later on the ground that they were close followers of the Commu-nist line.

The end of the war found Kagawa, like Japan itself, ex-hausted and stunned. But he gave himself immediately to rallying the scattered Japanese Christian community, to overseeing relief projects, establishing refugee camps and orphanages, to helping write the chauvinism out of school texts. And he went up and down the land on incessant tours of evangelism, feeling that never in history had there been such a chance to Christianize Japan.

Today, almost blind from trachoma (contracted during his work in the Kobe slums) and never wholly free from pain, Kagawa is nevertheless overflowing with energy and ideas. His books are again best sellers. His co-ops are stronger and more active than ever before. He directs three factories turning out products for his co-ops, and has estab-lished dozens of schools for workers. He sees in such factories much of Japan's economic hope for the future, and is every-where promoting small-scale manufacture, winter industry for rural people, decentralization of urban industry.

Thus this diminutive giant is still preaching to millions his gospel of love and brotherhood and co-operation. To men and nations he offers his formula for rich and worthy living. Rule One is: "Give yourself, freely and without re-serve, to the service of others."

He has no Rule Two.

XII

Chinese Refugees' Best Friend

The history of mankind reflects no principle more strongly than this: The most potent force on earth for world betterment is still *one-man power*. Just trace back to its source any monumental good in life and see how often you come to one person who, confronting some need, had the gumption and imagination to do something about it—on his own, and without any backing save the shove of his own compassion. And one of the most striking examples of this I know is a man named Gus Borgeest of Sunshine Island, near Hong Kong.

I first heard of the incredible Gus while prowling recently through the refugee-ridden city of Hong Kong. "A queer duck, Gus," said one of my informants. "Worries about people." In Hong Kong 670,000 refugees are jammed into tiny, disease-breeding cubicles, or sleep in the streets, or huddle hopelessly in tar paper shacks—firetraps without water, sewers or light. More than 300,000 can find no work, are dependent upon emergency relief supplied by over-burdened government and private welfare agencies.

When I asked: Is nobody trying to find more permanent solutions? I began to hear one answer: "Well, there's Gus Borgeest." It was plain that he was something of a legend. Faced with staggering human misery, he refused to wail limply, "What can one man do?" He went out and did it. Singlehanded and with his own slender funds, he set the pattern for a government-sponsored rural resettlement scheme that has brought rehabilitation to many refugee families and promises hope for many more.

I went in search of the man behind the legend. A choppy ride aboard a leaky sampan brought me to Sunshine Island, seven miles west of Hong Kong. Gus was standing on the beach, barefooted and sun-bronzed, and looking like a modern Crusoe in shorts and a floppy white hat.

"Welcome to the 'Isle of Hope'!" he shouted.

It seemed to be just that. In striking contrast to Hong Kong's squatter areas, the island was a humming, happy beehive of activity. Whole families were at work in gardens, harvesting cabbages, spinach, eggplant, sweet potatoes. Others were shaping terraces up the rocky hillsides, putting out fruit trees; still others were herding goats or tending flocks of ducks.

At that time 23 families, comprising 110 persons, were on the island. In a few weeks they would be ready for resettlement on farms of their own on the mainland, and newcomers would arrive from the squatter camps to learn how to turn "marginal" land into productive acres. All had been drawn from the worst of the squatter camps, or had sailed their sampans out of Red China via Macau. While I was there, a small boat bearing a man and wife, four children and grandmother and all their possessions arrived after a hazardous escape from the Communists; they were warmly welcomed and assigned garden plots.

A barefoot ball of fire, Gus Borgeest bounded through the hills and valleys of his domain, shedding vitality with every step. Tagging him breathlessly, I thought how aptly he had been described in Hong Kong: "a Simon Legree whose whip is a vision of hope."

Gus Borgeest has known and loved the Chinese all his life, hates fiercely the inhuman forces that have swept them into chains. Born in Shanghai, he is the son of a British-subject adventurer whose scrambled ancestry goes back to the Italian noble family, Borghese. For 20 years, until the Japanese took Shanghai in 1943, Gus worked as a production expediter in a British textile factory. During his two-year internment that followed, a book by Rufus Jones fell into his hands. The great American Quaker's urgings toward love and brotherhood fired Gus with what Quakers call a "concern" of his own for the poor and oppressed. Released in 1945, he joined the Society of Friends, took as his motto "My neighbor is my business!"

Gus and his wife Mona were helping impoverished Chinese families set up cottage industries when the Communists moved in and expelled him. Arriving in Hong Kong in 1951 with two Hong Kong dollars (about 34 cents), Gus found work with the government's Vegetable Marketing Organization and Social Welfare Office. This gave him a closeup of the refugees' plight. Many, he learned, were farmers who had abandoned land their families had farmed for centuries, in deep revulsion against Mao Tse-tung's "agrarian reforms." Centuries of misgovernment, even the Japanese invasion, had not been enough to make them quit their homes on lands their ancestors had farmed. Yet here they were—in the thousands.

He and Mona spent their spare time roving through the squatters' camps, talking to the refugees. "What haunted me most," Gus says, "was what the years of dependence upon charity was doing to their self-respect. Welfare, with the best of intentions, was subtly enslaving them, as handouts always do." He began to preach the self-help route to rehabilitation. "It's never been beaten," he says, "either as an economic measure or as a restorer of human dignity."

Only land to farm would make these refugees contented members of society. But where was land? Colony officials, long inured to frustration, viewed Gus's concern sympathetically but without hope. But one who listened with hopeful curiosity was K. M. A. Barnett, District Commissioner for the New Territories, a hilly area on the Chinese mainland which was leased from China under an 1898 treaty. But, as Barnett pointed out, most of it comprised rocky hillsides or abandoned acres. And these were already supporting 300,000 people. The remaining 305 square miles not taken by farms and by the cities of Hong Kong and Kowloon were nothing but rocky hillsides, barren islands or abandoned acres in the New Territories. "Marginal land, we call it," said Barnett. "But I'm afraid it is over the margin!"

Gus asked, "If I can find a spot to demonstrate that refugees can be trained to make marginal land productive, will the government provide land to resettle them?"

Barnett smiled. "Of course, Mr. Borgeest. But what background do you have to teach farming?"

Gus grinned. "Twenty years in a textile factory!"

A few days later, returning from a mercy visit to a nearby island leper colony, Gus and Mona passed a small abandoned atoll which showed signs of having once been farmed. He beached his sampan, paced its 160 acres. The soil was poor, but active springs betokened an adequate water supply. Excitedly he called to his wife, "Mona, this is it!"

While negotiating for the island, Gus pored over books on marginal-land farming, plagued experts in the Agriculture Department, took counsel from everybody except those who advised him to forget his dream. Finally, in May 1953, government officials agreed to let him have the island for an annual rental of HK$ 148. "We hate to take your money, Gus," they said. "Nobody can grow anything but failure on that barren land."

Less than a week later Borgeest packed his wife, their five-year-old daughter Naomi and two refugee farmers aboard a rented sampan and headed for Sunshine Island. The passengers were wedged in between equipment—tents, cots, a few tools, food for a week—which had eaten severely into the $700 he had saved during two frugal years as a government employe. The first night on the island, four inches of rain fell, but the next morning Gus and the two men set out for the fields.

When a fisherman and his family, escapees from Communist China, put into the island and asked for asylum, Gus's transport problem was simplified. Soon he took to shuttling back and forth between the island and Hong Kong, adding a few goats, chickens, geese and rabbits with each trip.

All able-bodied adults put in eight hours in the fields or helping construct housing. Evening discussions dealt with farm techniques, sanitation and health, civic responsibility. Each family was given a thatched hut, beds, soap, three meals a day—plus HK$ 50 a month. The wage did wonders for the spirit of people who had not earned a dollar in years. And hope and hard work in the sun did wonders for their health.

Before accepting any family, Gus made it plain that Sunshine Island was no haven for the lazy. Two virtues were needed: "yearning for a farm of your own, and a willingness to work hard." He carefully selected only those who could adapt themselves to the toil and exposure.

The early months were not easy. A typhoon roared across the island, ripping off roofs, blowing away the community kitchen, destroying goat houses and rabbit hutches. Gus viewed the setback as a disguised blessing. "It brought much needed rain for our gardens," he proclaimed, "and a forceful warning that we must rebuild more adequately."

He promptly laid out plans for stone instead of thatched houses. Only after all his families were settled in sturdy new homes did he and Mona construct their own rough stone cottage, grandly naming it "Villa Borghese."

Gus's savings were soon gone.

"Faith was the only operating capital we had," he says. He set the women to cutting bundles of dry grass, to sell in Hong Kong for fuel. He sold rabbits and poultry. After two months his garden plots were producing enough vegetables for the island. In four months he was saying, "Now I know it can be done!"

As word of his valiant fight spread, individuals contributed funds and supplies, offered him interest-free loans until the island could be made self-supporting. The loans he paid back meticulously, and to all contributors he rendered a minutely detailed statement of income and expenditures.

"I'm finding," he said, "that if you obligate yourself for God's children, God will somehow provide." That did not mean idly waiting for miracles. "We can't expect manna from heaven every 20 minutes; God expects us to do our part first."

When he ran out of money he ran out to tell more people about Sunshine Island. Intrigued by his optimism, civic clubs, social workers, newsmen and others began coming to Sunshine Island. Proudly Gus displayed the gardens and herds, the busy people in the fields. Students from Chinese refugee colleges formed work camps, came to the island to dig fish ponds, irrigation ditches and water reservoirs. A contingent of Royal Air Force men gave long week-ends to helping out.

When social agencies showed interest, Gus told them: "Why not apply some of your relief funds to sponsoring a family for training here?" And so the "family sponsorship" plan got under way. The cost: $27 a month, including the wage paid. Soon individuals, churches and welfare agencies were offering to sponsor families.

First to respond to his "family sponsorship" plan was Colonel Fred Waller of the Salvation Army, who sent two families (both are now successfully farming their own acres in the New Territories). Others were sponsored by individuals, one by the Hong Kong welfare society. Most were successes in rehabilitation.

But not all. Despite the most careful screening, Gus drew some duds. Some families, with the best of intentions, could not adapt themselves to his tough regimen. These he sent packing. Others had been too long at the public feeding-trough to resurrect their ambition. "It's a pity," he told Mona, "but we can't help people like that."

Kindly and helpful to the industrious, he was trigger-tempered with any who slacked, often had to tell himself "not to be so caustic but to pipe down and be more diplomatic."

To compound his difficulties, the government dragged its feet in finding land suitable for resettling the trainees. After more than a year on the island, four of his more promising families became impatient and left in a body.

Not so discouraging were the number who stayed on the island long enough to build up their health and self-reliance, then left to carve out their own future. One, Teng Foo Sang, acquired enough know-how to take a job as supervisor of a large farm owned by a relative. Others were snapped up by agricultural interests. A fisher family who had fled Red China, its faith in free enterprise restored, earned enough to buy a new boat and joined Hong Kong's big fishing fleet at Aberdeen.

One of Borgeest's side projects, not strictly related to prospective farmers, was his rehabilitation of drug addicts, attempted suicides, post-tuberculosis cases, cured lepers in need of reorientation before facing again the society that had banned them.

Visiting a Hong Kong hospital one day, Gus was shown a little tailor. Fleeing Communist China, the man had lost his family and possessions and, finding no work in Hong Kong, had tried to poison himself. When the hospital almoner said, "I hate to release this poor fellow; he'll only try again to kill himself," Gus replied, "Let me take him." He put the man to work weeding the gardens, doing odd jobs, gradually pumped new hope into his mind. After six months, the tailor was set up in his own shop in a village in the New Territories, happy and prospering. Says Gus:

"Contact with friendliness, good food and the good earth turned the trick."

Another would-be suicide, a formerly prosperous sugar merchant from Shanghai who had lost his family to the Communists, also received the successful Borgeest treatment; he was soon completely rehabilitated.

Drug addicts were tougher to rehabilitate. With dope plentiful in Hong Kong, many disheartened refugees turned to it for release from their misery. Gus's prescription for those who wished to conquer the habit: "Hard work, sweat and sleep—in that order."

Those who took his cure found it worked. For example, there was the stevedore who had lost both his job and his family because of opium-smoking. Desperate, he paddled seven miles to the island, told Borgeest, "I *must* master this thing!" Gus assigned him to the heaviest work he had, digging irrigation ditches from early morning till dark. The man stayed three months, gradually sweated the poison from his system. He became a skilled farmer, producing more and better products than any other, and now is happily settled, with his family, on a farm of his own.

Another case was an elderly lady, 20 years an addict. Her daughter, a student nurse in a Kowloon hospital, said, "She shames me," begged Gus to accept her on the island. Bluntly Gus told the mother, "You must promise to stay here for six months and work hard every waking minute."

The old lady snapped, "This is jail! I go back."

Gus shrugged, "As you like, madam. We have no police; nobody will stop you. But if you go, I've told your daughter to have no more to do with you."

The old lady mulled it over, finally said, "All right. I

stay." She did—for over a year; conquered her habit, eventually paid her own board and lodging. At her daughter's graduation, they clasped each other, said in the same breath, "I'm so proud of you!"

Gus's remarkable success with such cases could have changed the whole character of his work, if he had let it. Special welfare agencies, swamped with maladjusted persons, continually besought him for help. His reply: "I'm glad to take them when we have room. But I must stick to my original purpose—resettling refugees. I've got a point to prove!"

By September 1954, after an almost superhuman struggle to keep his project alive, Gus received word that his success had been closely observed in Hong Kong. Private and public agencies had devised a sweeping refugee program based on three points: (1) financing, (2) training of refugees, (3) permanent resettlement. Sunshine Island, which had showed the way, was to be the prime implementer of the second point.

Church World Service, backed by funds from Americans, was first to act, placing 11 sponsored families on the island for six months' training. The United Church of Canada sent $1000.

With every private gift or unexpected bonanza he brought in another family or introduced a new planting project. When a cynical friend groused that "you're wasting your time trying to help those down-and-out refugees," Gus took him to the island, showed him what was going on—and the doubter left behind him enough money to put in a grove of 1000 papaya trees.

Meanwhile the government speeded its survey of land

available for resettlement. To his friends and sponsors, Gus sent out a lilting bulletin: "What we have been struggling toward for so long is about to come to fruition . . ." On Sunshine Island new housing and gardens, orchards, water systems and fish ponds sprang into being. With his refugees now wresting rich harvests from the unpromising soil, the "island earnings" item in his reports showed a sharp upturn. When sponsors objected that nothing was charged out for "administration," Gus voted the Borgeests a salary of $33 a month—and promptly put it back into the island kitty under "anonymous donation."

To be sure his trainees would have a place to go, he constantly needled Colony officials to complete their survey of resettlement acreage, spent days traipsing through the New Territories, conferring with village elders in likely sites.

By the end of February 1956 the first group of sponsored trainees, with other families he had nourished on his own, were ready for resettlement on government-selected land in the New Territories—a plateau called Cheung Sheung. Two acres were set aside for each family, and each was supplied with a cow, farm and domestic equipment, seed and fertilizer and a small cash allowance.

Like a tough but solicitous top sergeant curious to know his squad's battlefitness after rugged basic training, Gus accompanied the families to Cheung Sheung, helped them get settled, went back weekly to check their progress.

Even he could not expect more. In a few weeks they had their acres cleared and tilled, orchards planted, permanent stone houses built, and were eating their fill from food their own hands had coaxed from the rocky soil.

Moreover, the newcomers revived hope in the area's old

settlers. Eager to keep up with the new Joneses, many of these fell upon their fields with renewed zeal. One who had been on the verge of heeding Communist pressure to move to Red China, said, "My new neighbors' example made me lose face. The fault was not in the land but in me." Today he is Cheung Sheung's ablest exponent of "capitalistic farming."

Under Gus's direction the settlers created their own village organization to represent them before the government. Their first victory: winning the promise that their acres, for which they paid a rental of HK$ 8 a year, would become theirs forever after 10 years of successful occupancy.

In May, 1956, Hong Kong's governor, Sir Alexander Grantham, visited Cheung Sheung and was amazed at what he saw. He and his staff plied Gus with questions, began to wonder if marginal-land farming might not be the most encouraging answer to the refugee problem. They estimated that Hong Kong Colony, for all its limited space, could in time resettle at least 1000 families.

District Commissioner Barnett told me, "There is a Chinese fable about an old man who had to cross a hill every day. Each day he took a stone in each hand from the top of the hill to the bottom. Asked why, he said, 'I'm moving this hill. Not in my lifetime, perhaps not in my son's, but in time, by doing what we can, this hill will be gone.' That's the lesson Gus Borgeest has taken to heart.

"Our problem, as Gus sees it, is a problem of human beings and of the earth. Neither submits easily to master plans, but both respond to love and tender care. Hasn't Gus proved that his approach succeeds where more ambitious schemes may fail?"

One of the new settlers gravely told the governor: "Sir, owning one's own land, managing one's own affairs, does something to a man. Such cannot be achieved, or even understood, by those who are content to let the government fill their rice bowls for them."

One of the many Americans who have visited Sunshine Island is Prof. Theodore Herman of Colgate University. He reports: "Sunshine Island is such a small drop in a vast sea of despair that it may seem to have no measurable impact on the refugee problem. But I keep remembering that every vision and act that has caught the allegiance of others *began with one person*—not with a committee, a society, or a congregation. Sunshine Island by itself may never solve the refugee problem anywhere, but if Gus can keep going financially and physically, his demonstration of faith in that part of God within every man might convince more humans to do likewise—or even to help solve human problems before they cause more refugees.

"Gus Borgeest does not differ from most of us in believing that God calls us to a life of loving service. He does differ from most of us in having acted on that belief."

XIII

Through Gates of Splendor

On January 9, 1956, teletypes in newsrooms all over the world began clacking out the first fragmentary accounts of one of the most daring Christian missionary exploits of modern times.

Reported missing were five young American missionaries who, deep in Ecuador's tangled jungles, had been carrying out a secret and ingeniously planned campaign to make friendly contact with one of the most savage Stone Age tribes left on earth—the Auca Indians. Three days before, they had made that contact, the first white men ever to do so. They had radioed their base, "This is a great day for the advance of the gospel in Ecuador!"

A few days later, when rescue parties finally reached the camp the missionaries had set up on a Curaray River beach in the heart of Auca territory, the five bodies were found—pierced by spears and strewn like driftwood amid the river's debris. On their bodies and scattered over the shambled beach were water-soaked diaries detailing their adventure.

The story, occupying front pages for days, quickly took on the flavor of an epic. It was an inspiring reminder that the peculiar power and God-given courage which historically have spread Christianity to earth's every remote corner are still very much alive. And still triumphant.

228

"Operation Auca," as the five had dubbed it, began on a brilliantly clear day back in September 1955, when the pilot of a Protestant missionary air group serving a string of jungle mission stations in Ecuador took off on an emergency call. The missionary at Arajuno had radioed that he had a sick Quechua Indian boy and needed an injection syringe—fast.

As he swung his tiny plane away from his base at Shell Mera, 100 miles south of Quito in the Andes foothills, Nate Saint noted with satisfaction the unusual clearness of the sky. Visibility, normally much limited by haze, was at least 75 miles—an ideal day to go exploring.

Thirty minutes of flying brought him to the pencil-thin slash in the jungle that was the Arajuno station. Strapping young Ed McCully, in charge there, was waiting for him. A football and track star back at Wheaton College in Illinois, McCully had been president of his senior class, and was studying law at Marquette when he felt called to missionary service.

Ed grinned. "Sorry, Nate," he said. "Looks like I brought you out here for nothing. Emergency's past."

Nate shrugged; it was all in the day's work. But when the routine supplies and mail were unloaded, he pulled McCully aside from the Quechuas milling about the plane.

"Say, Ed," he whispered, "how about going to look for 'the neighbors'?" McCully's brow went up. "Right!" he said eagerly.

"The neighbors" were the Aucas, a tribe so vicious that even the head-hunting Jivaros feared to enter their territory. Exactly where and how they lived, nobody knew for sure. Books and articles mentioning them were a confusion of contradictions. Well known, however, was the fact that they hated all strangers, that they went through the jungle like vengeful wraiths, flinging their needle-sharp hardwood spears with deadly accuracy, spreading terror among other tribes. Masters of ambush, they had a long and bloody record of killings.

The government left the Aucas severely alone; attempts to reach them had cost too many lives. Only missionaries felt any urge to get near them. But among the missionaries the desire to win the Aucas had for years been a passionate pre-occupation. To Christian pioneers who took seriously the command "Go ye . . . to every creature," the Aucas' very unreachability, as well as their "lostness" without Christian light, was a continuing challenge.

Neither Nate Saint nor Ed McCully had any idea how the tribe could be reached. On hundreds of flights to the mission stations he served Nate had searched in vain for some sign of Auca habitation. But now, on a crystal-clear day like this . . .

Nate and Ed leapt into the Piper and took off. They headed east for 50 miles, then north toward the Napo, one of the Amazon's headwaters. Faces pressed against the plexiglass, they peered down into the endless stretches of jungle, eagerly alert.

Suddenly, just as their gas was getting low, Nate caught sight of a blemish in the jungle pattern. The blemish grew into a well-defined pockmark, then into a good-sized clearing. He nudged McCully, jabbed a forefinger downward. Circling, they counted 15 small clearings and as many houses. It was the first Auca settlement they had ever seen, and it left them breathless with elation.

A few days later they confided their find to two other young missionaries: Jim Elliot, whose station was at Shandia, and Pete Fleming at Puyu Pungu. Both had shared the "Auca dream" with Saint and McCully.

On September 29 Nate made four other exploratory flights, hoping to find a settlement nearer Arajuno. On one he took along two Quechua Indian guides, not telling them the purpose of the flight. Suddenly while zigzagging through a jungle valley he spotted some clearings, drifted down for a closer look. The Indians immediately cried, "Aucas!" Terror tinged their voices.

To himself Nate said exultantly, "This is it!"

By October 1 he had made enough trips over the region to mark the spot as unquestionably a sizable Auca settlement—and only 15 minutes by air from Arajuno. That night the young missionaries got together at Shell Mera and sprawled on the living-room floor with a big map spread out before them. They had decided that "the Lord's time" had come to do something more than talk and dream about contacting the Aucas.

The excited planning went on most of the night and produced some firm decisions. The first was: strict secrecy. They would finance the project from their own pockets, not draw on mission funds. Only members of the team and wives were to be in the know. Their reasons were sound: if word of the operation got abroad, droves of explorers and adventurers, newsmen and photographers might try to get into the act. Then at the first sign of Auca hostility someone would start shooting—"and set back the missionary effort among these people for decades."

There had been tragic precedents which made the mis-

sionaries wary of joining forces with men who had no love
or special regard for the Aucas. Five years before, an expe-
dition led by a Swedish explorer and a Columbia scientist—
accompanied by newspaper fanfare and employing a missionary guide—had come to grief. As the party approached on
their balsa rafts, it was ambushed at a narrow bend in the
river. At first sight of the Aucas, a Quechua porter had
opened fire. Several in the party had been wounded when
the Aucas routed it with flying spears.

To further insure secrecy the five young missionaries devised code terms, for use when others were around or when
communicating over the missions' short-wave radios. The
Aucas were to be called "the neighbors," their region "the
neighborhood." The Auca settlement was to be "Terminal
City"; the beach where the missionaries would land and set
up the contact camp, "Palm Beach." Moreover, each man
would carry on his regular mission work up to the last minute to avoid arousing curiosity among the Indians and other
missionaries.

To soften up Auca hostility, they would start with a long,
cautious campaign of air-borne friendliness. Regular weekly
flights would be made over the Auca village, low enough
to drop gifts and shout friendly greetings but high enough
to outrange Auca spears. For that, the small Piper Family
Cruiser would be ideal.

"The Shell Company people once tried dropping gifts,"
Nate commented. "But the Aucas, apparently scared by the
2000-horsepower transport roaring over at low level, threw
lances at the plane. Captive Aucas later explained that they
thought the gifts fell from the plane's stomach as a result of
being wounded by the lances."

For bestowing their gifts Nate had developed a tricky technique. He called it "the spiraling-line method." After long search for some simple way of making a sustained air-ground contact, he discovered it one day in 1500 feet of fishing line and a small canvas bucket. Experimentally paying out the line while circling at 1000 feet, he found to his amazement that he could make the bucket hang vertically and almost motionless. Then, by gradually spiraling lower, he could set it down with reasonable accuracy. He had already used this method for lowering medicines and mail to jungle clearings, and for picking up messages from missionaries on the trail.

Once he had astounded a missionary in a remote jungle village by lowering a field telephone in the canvas bucket. The village was being swept by a highly contagious disease, and when the incredulous missionary picked up the telephone Nate asked for details of the situation. Then, using his plane radio, he called a mission hospital 150 miles away, asked for diagnosis and instructions, and lowered the prescribed medicines then and there. The whole operation took a matter of minutes—and the epidemic was stopped.

This simple "life line from the skies" had proved a great boon to mission outposts. Now it seemed to be "God's answer" for Operation Auca.

But how about communication with the Aucas? So far as was known, there was only one member of the tribe available who remembered the language—a girl named Dayuma, who years before had fled from the tribe after seeing her father, brother and baby sister hacked to death in an intertribal row. The girl knew the Quechua tongue, so Jim and Betty Elliot, who spoke it fluently, were assigned to assemble from her a stock of Auca words and phrases, then drill the others in their usage.

The first gift drop was scheduled for Thursday, October 6.

To understand their powerful compulsion to reach the hitherto unreached with the Gospel—or die in the attempt —it is necessary to know these men more intimately.

Nathaniel Saint, at 32, was the "old man" of the group. Also, he had been longest in Ecuador: seven years. He received a thorough religious training from his father, Lawrence B. Saint, noted muralist and stained-glass artist. Significantly, Nate had been his father's model for the window in Washington's National Cathedral depicting a small boy bringing his loaves and fishes to Christ for the feeding of the multitude. At 13, stricken with osteomyelitis, young Nate promised God that "if He would let me live, my life would henceforth belong to Him." Recovered, he kept his bargain.

Planes early became his passion. In high school he worked afternoons and Saturdays to earn money for flying lessons, and during World War II he served in the U.S. Air Force. When he went to Wheaton College to prepare himself for foreign-mission service his only regret was that it meant forsaking his first love—flying. Then one day news came that some ex-service airmen in California had formed a group called the Missionary Aviation Fellowship, and were recruiting pilots who were also mechanics for air supply-line service to missionaries in bush and jungle. To Nate the news was the voice of God. He dropped his college course and hurried to California. "The Lord called me from aviation to Himself," he said later—"and then sent me back to aviation for Himself!"

The Missionary Aviation Fellowship needed a man to pioneer its program in Ecuador. Nate, with his wife Marjorie, flew down in September 1948, established a base for his small plane at Shell Mera, on the edge of the jungle. He soon had a network of landing strips and radio communications (with Marj at the base radio hookup and in touch with him constantly), and in a matter of months had transformed life for the mission stations. Where missionaries once had been isolated and remote, sometimes bedridden for weeks with jungle diseases, they now were within a half hour's flying time of transportation between stations or ambulance service, and got quick delivery of mail, medicines, supplies.

Nate developed extraordinary skill in getting in and out of jungle airstrips, many scarcely wide enough to keep his wing tips from brushing the trees. He had no illusions about the dangers of such jungle-hopping. "Every time I take off," he said, "I am ready to deliver up the life I owe to God." He came close to delivering it up one day when, in taking off from the Quito airport, a sudden downdraft from the mountains hurled his light Stinson plane to the ground. In the crash his back was broken, his eyes blinded. Yet, when his sight returned a few weeks later, he hastened back to his work while still encased from neck to thighs in a cast. Meanwhile, from his hospital bed, lest his accident prove a setback for missionary aviation he had made a tape-recording for the people back home:

"It's only logical," he told them, "for conservatives to say, 'Let's quit this foolish risk of life.' They would see it differently if they knew the chances taken for God every day by these missionaries in the jungle. We in missionary aviation must always take the safest and sanest course, never being reckless. But we cannot be less courageous than these brave people in the field."

Nate Saint had his theories on expendability, learned during the war. "God Himself set the pattern," he said, "and if He did not hold back His own Son, why should we hold back our own little lives for the sake of security? We are—and must always be—expendable." And in his diary he wrote, "The Aucas kill on sight, but someone must take the Gospel to them. Beyond their territory are other souls for whom Christ died."

Like Nate Saint, the others were young, full of vigor and spiritual drive. There was nothing ascetic or anti-life about them. In college all had been campus leaders, top scholars, better-than-average athletes.

Jim Elliot, Peter Fleming and Ed McCully had many things in common. They were all products of homes where religious faith was daily bread and spreading the Gospel a divine duty; they were members of the same fellowship (Plymouth Brethren), arrived in Ecuador the same year (1952), were sponsored by the same foreign-missions group (Christian Missions in Many Lands).

Before coming to Ecuador this trio's paths had crossed often, as youth leaders on campus and in Christian youth activity. They developed a common feeling for Latin America as a place to invest their lives, and all felt, soon after arrival in Ecuador, a God-impelled urge to "get to" the Aucas.

Of the three, Jim Elliot was first to contract "the Ecuador itch," and shortly passed the enthusiasm along. Unusually handsome and well-built, and only 28 when he died, he had an exuberant zest for living. "Wherever you are, be *all* there," he once wrote; "live to the hilt every situation you believe to be the will of God." At Wheaton College he was a champion wrestler, a star debater and public speaker, the outstanding spiritual leader on campus, and he graduated with highest honors. He went to Ecuador in February 1952, and there later married Betty Howard, daughter of a former missionary.

At jungle mission stations, first at Puyu Pungu, then at Shandia on the banks of the Napo River, Jim and Betty not only spread the Gospel but in addition did medical and first-aid work: splinting broken arms, treating malaria and snake bites, teaching the Quechuas sanitation. They also compiled textbooks in the Quechua tongue, then taught the Quechuas to read and write their own language.

But Jim Elliot was preoccupied with the Aucas, and had frankly talked over with Betty the hazards of reaching them. He loved life, had once written effusively, "I love thee, Life —not because thou art long but because I have thee from God." He had often preached to his Quechuas, *"When it comes time to die, make sure that all you have to do is die!"* The last entry in his diary read: "God, send me soon to the Aucas."

Youngest of the team was Peter Fleming—only 27 when he died on the Curaray beach. Fervently religious, he was more introspective than the others. He had an impressive knowledge of the Bible. Beside his picture in his high-school yearbook he put this slogan: "I don't know what the future holds—but I know Who holds the future." At the University of Washington he was an honor student. He loved the language sciences, in 1951 took his M.A. in English. At his mission station at Puyu Pungu he quickly mastered the

Quechua dialects, and with his wife, Olive, had a lively literacy program going among the Indians.

But Pete, too, became intensely interested in getting to the Aucas. In college he had been a conscientious objector, seeing no way to reconcile the Christian doctrine of love with the killing of one human being by another. Yet he had no fear of death for himself; his dedication to Operation Auca was complete.

Of the four, Ed McCully had the best reasons for sober second thoughts over the Auca enterprise. For over a year he and his wife, Marilou, had been working with the Quechuas at Arajuno—on the very doorstep of Auca-land. Arajuno was an old Shell Oil camp, abandoned when it was found that more blood than oil flowed from the site.

The Auca attacks did not subside with Arajuno's switch from oil to Gospel base. To lessen the danger, McCully had cleared the jungle growth back from the mission house, erected an electric fence to discourage raiders, put up a battery-operated light that could flood the area at first sound of approach. Yet, despite all these precautions, a half dozen Quechuas had been slain by the Aucas during his stay. It was the Aucas' hostility, in fact, that made Ed McCully anxious to reach them with news of God's love.

Such, then, were the men who, in a spirit lifted right out of the Acts of the Apostles, fashioned their bold odyssey to the Aucas.

They were not perfect, these men. They freely acknowledged their weaknesses and foibles. Nate Saint had his battles with frustration, Pete Fleming his bouts with a tendency toward too-hasty judgment of others. Jim Elliot was prone to plunging in where angels feared to tread—not

Gus Borgeest, indomitable Quaker, stands on the shore of his "isle of hope" in Hong Kong to welcome another family of escapees arriving by sampan from Communist China. (Chapter XII)

Borgeest inspects a vegetable field on Sunshine Island, where refugee Chinese find a haven and a new life.

Jim Elliot

Pete Fleming

A month before landing on the Curaray River deep in the Auca territory of Ecuador, the participants in Operation Auca were introduced to the savage tribe by photographs dropped from the missionary plane. The "insignia of the operation," a sketch of the yellow Piper Cruiser, appeared on the pictures, and the missionaries were photographed holding gifts received earlier from the Indians. (Chapter XIII)

Ed McCully

Roger Youderian

Nate Saint

always pausing to consider whether the angels had good ground for their fears. Ed McCully fought "pride of accomplishment" and "thoughts of sin" which, he found, "Satan is ever ready to inject at every idle moment, perhaps right at the close of a very intimate period with God."

But if they were not perfect, neither were they petty. In all the accounts of Operation Auca there is no hint of any jousting for leadership, any panting for preferment, any pouting over position. Their consecration to their task was constant. And they were eager to profit from any mistakes as they went along. As Nate Saint put it: "If we humbly seek His will in any matter, crucifying our own desires, and venture by faith and not in fear, we can't go wrong."

It was with high faith, and not fear, that Nate Saint and Ed McCully took off from Arajuno, early on October 6, to make their first gift drop. On the Arajuno strip Ed was waiting—with the first gift for the Aucas, a small aluminum kettle with a lid. Inside were about 20 brightly colored buttons —"obviously not for their clothes, since they don't wear any, but they do make good ornaments." Having read that the Aucas had no salt sources of their own, Nate insisted on adding a little sack of rock salt. "If they know what the stuff is good for, we're sure to make friends." To the gifts they attached some yard-long streamers, brightly colored.

They loaded their emergency equipment, rigged the special gift-drop gear, made a test run to be sure they could get the rig overboard—and took off. In 15 minutes they were over "Terminal City." Keeping to the downstream edge of the Auca territory so that if they had a forced landing they could escape by water, they eventually found a cluster of

buildings that interested them: a large thatched house surrounded by several smaller ones. "The main house," Nate
reported later, "was about 40 yards from the stream, fronting
a sand bar perhaps 75 yards long and 15 yards wide. A path
showed they used this bar frequently—it would be our
target. There was not a living person in sight."

Nate slowed to 55 m.p.h. while Ed lowered the gift over
the side. It was an aluminum kettle, to which were attached
some yard-long, brightly colored streamers. The line dropped
straight and clear, and Nate began circling. The gift drifted
in a small, lazy circle below them, the ribbons fluttering
nicely.

There was still no sign of life below. "If no one's watching," Ed shouted, "we'd better put it in an obvious place."

They started spiraling down. There was considerable wind
drift from the north, and the hills behind the stream were
covered with tall trees. They made six attempts, gradually
lifting the bucket against the wind until it was over the bar.
Then Nate rolled into a steeper turn and the gift hit the
beach right on the path to the main house.

The automatic release mechanism Nate had developed
worked perfectly, the line floated free—"and there was our
messenger of good will, love and faith, below us on the
sand bar! We had delivered the first Gospel message by sign
language to a people a quarter of a mile away vertically,
50 miles horizontally, but continents and wide seas away
culturally and spiritually."

Back home, exuberant at their success, Nate and Ed met
some good-humored skepticism when they confessed they
hadn't seen a soul. Were they sure they hadn't deposited the
gift in a deserted village? But the pair's enthusiasm was

damp-proof. They knew that, at long last, a start had been made.

Their second trip, a week later, dispelled any notion that Terminal City was without habitants. They immediately checked the sand bar where they had left their first offering. The kettle was gone.

This time the gift was a new machete—an item so coveted by the Aucas that they had killed to get it—and their target a house upstream from the first one. "We figured that if we specialized on any one house, the others might get jealous." When they got to the target-house, they spotted four canoes pulled up on the riverbank in front of it. Obviously, someone must be nearby.

They began circling and Ed lowered the machete, which was canvas-wrapped so that no one would be cut, and decked with gay streamers. Ed watched its descent through binoculars. Suddenly, as Nate described it later, "He let out a yell and all but crawled out the open door to get a better look. *We were seeing our first Auca.* He was running around but not hiding. Pretty soon there were three of them out in front of their big leaf house."

They could see the Aucas watching the dangling gift as it came down. The machete fell into the stream, and instantly an Auca dived for it. Soon half a dozen of them were on the bank examining the prize. Apparently the gift idea had caught on in a hurry.

There was other evidence that "the neighbors" were interested. Back at Arajuno, Nate and Ed found the Quechuas milling about excitedly. They had found in the brush near Ed's house a number of footprints, obviously Aucas'. Said Ed, "Could be that these came from Terminal City, after our first visit." Said Nate, "They probably hid out there in the brush to look you over last night!"

Immediately the two fell to work making a wooden model of the plane, put it on a pole outside the McCully house, to identify for any future visitors McCully's connection with the operation.

Their third visit a week later revealed larger numbers of Aucas, increased excitement among them—and no signs of fear. Coming down to a lower altitude than before, Nate circled each of the four main houses of the village while Ed snapped pictures of the Aucas running up and down the stream bed laughing and shouting, apparently trying to guess where the gift drop would be made this time.

A snappy northeast wind made accurate spotting of the machete difficult. Several times when the gift was lowering near them, the Aucas would scramble helter-skelter in that direction, then off to another as it drifted out of reach. They laughed and shouted, obviously considering it a game.

Finally, after a couple of near misses, Ed set the machete down within 10 feet of the main house's front door. The Aucas had it immediately, holding to the line for several minutes while untying the machete. Ed shouted, "Hey, get this thrill—holding onto a line held on the other end by an Auca!" Nate rolled out of a turn and reached over, gave the line a couple of light tugs. "Man, that's fishing!" he shouted back.

The line pulled in, they circled down lower than they had been before. The idea was to fly past the Aucas to give them a close look at their faces—for purposes of identification later. At 200 feet they tossed out a piece of ribbon, "and a brown man had it like a spider takes a fly." A few of the villagers ran for cover as the plane came so low, but reappeared waving as the Piper circled slowly higher and higher before leaving the site.

The two returned home jubilant. "May God continue to put His good hand on this project," Nate wrote in his diary that night, "and may we abandon it when not fully assured of His direction. At present we feel unanimously that God is in it."

Now they were prepared to try out verbal communication. Nate rigged up a public-address system in the plane, and Jim Elliot, who had drilled himself in Auca phrases learned from Dayuma, the fugitive woman, went with Nate for the fourth visit.

Before making their gift drop they circled slowly over the settlement, while Jim called over the speaker, "We like you. We are your friends." This time they left several gifts—a machete, a ten-inch aluminum kettle filled with ribbons, trinkets, a shirt. The Indians converged on them with obvious delight, and one Auca cupped his hands as though calling something back. The missionaries were making faster progress than they had believed possible.

On the next trip their reception was even more favorable. McCully manned the mike to call out, "We like you. . . . We like you. . . . We have come to pay you a visit." The Aucas danced about eagerly, and though the plane came down low no one ran away, none showed the slightest fear. When Ed held out both hands in a gesture of open friendship, some of the Aucas imitated the gesture, shouting and smiling.

Thus encouraged, the team began to consider the next step—the actual landing in Auca territory, the face-to-face contact all had dreamed of. And from then on significant signs of friendliness were certainly not lacking.

On the sixth trip "the neighbors" received their gifts with great excitement, waving and yelling at the plane circling above. When Nate and Ed pulled in the line, they discovered that the Aucas had tied something on it. It was a beautifully woven headband, made of cord and brightly colored feathers. And on the next trip the Aucas sent up two sets of combs made of palmwood, whittled and woven intricately with native cord. Even more surprising was the appearance of a model airplane mounted atop one of the houses. Perhaps it was fashioned after secretly observing the model plane at Arajuno. In any case it indicated good will—and a craftsmanship hitherto unsuspected among such primitives.

The team noted the Aucas' reaction to bright colors. So they rifled their own wardrobes for the fanciest haberdashery available: a red-and-black checked shirt, gaudy shorts, red swimming trunks. These the Aucas donned upon delivery, and paraded proudly about the clearing. "These fellows," commented Nate wryly, "will be diked out like dudes before we get to meet them on the ground!"

To an elderly man who stalked like a potentate about a separate clearing of his own, accompanied always by two women, they dropped a T-shirt and a pair of Jim's pants. On the next trip Nate suggested, "Let's go by and see how the old boy liked his new pants." As the plane came over, the old man strode out into the clearing, clad in the pants and T-shirt, and saluted gravely. His wives stood stolidly by, dubiously eyeing their man's sartorial get-up. "One wore a baby, the other nothing," Nate noted.

The Aucas now even attempted to match the missionaries'

bounty in kind. When Nate and Ed sent down a live rooster, the Aucas came back the following week with a large black bird, and later sent up two parrots. When the missionaries lowered several small packages of food, the Aucas sent back cooked fish, packets of peanuts, a piece of smoked monkey tail.

The unique trading went on for another five weeks. To make their identity unmistakable, the team took photos of themselves wearing or holding the Auca gifts, made 6 x 9 enlargements tinted in lifelike colors. In the corner of each print they put the "insignia of the operation," a drawing of the yellow Piper, and dropped them along with their next gifts.

Meanwhile the Aucas, noting the difficulty of making drops among the tall trees, felled the trees around their houses to make clearings. Going even further, they erected large platforms about 15 feet from the ground—palpably to aid the missionaries in getting closer—stationed a "traffic director" on each, and here displayed their gifts for the pickup.

Shortly after this development Aucas appeared at Arajuno. Early one morning a mission Quechua named Fermín suddenly spotted one of them, naked and armed with a lance, at the end of the garden path. As they saw each other, the Auca ran away. Fermín dashed back to the mission and beat on Marilou McCully's window (she being alone there at the time save for Indian helpers), yelling for ammunition for his gun.

Marilou took the gun, which fortunately was not loaded, from Fermín's shaking hands. Then, with a machete for a gift, she headed down the path, calling in Auca phrases: "We like you. . . . We like you." Fermín came after her, shouting in Quechua, "You're crazy, you're crazy. They'll kill you!"

Around the path, freshly pressed grass indicated the recent presence of a number of Aucas. Marilou tossed the machete to the ground, called out more friendly phrases, and returned to her agitated flock. There was no doubt about it: Aucas were definitely around.

Nate and Ed, hastily summoned from other stations, flew in and saw in the visit a lost opportunity to contact the Aucas. They also realized that a shooting by one of the Quechuas would ruin all they had built up so far.

The incident underscored the desirability of making an early ground contact with the Aucas. Despite elaborate precautions to keep the operation secret, the Quechuas had by now shrewdly guessed what was going on. Two of them had even found one of the gift bags, and remarked testily, "Why you give all that good stuff to Aucas?" Their jealousy was aroused, and they would certainly gossip. Action was advisable before the secret leaked further through the jungle. And after nine increasingly successful gift drops the time seemed ripe.

Early in December Nate called the team together for a conference. They agreed that every consideration, including the weather, seemed to be catapulting them toward their D-day with now-or-never exigency. Within a month the rainy season would start, flooding the rivers and making landings impossible. The ideal time for establishing their beachhead in Auca-land would be early January during the full of the moon.

They set the date for Tuesday, January 3, 1956.

The only possible landing sites were sand beaches along the Curaray River. After days of exploration, Nate and Ed had found one that looked likely, some four miles from the Auca village. It was only about 200 yards long, and the approach and pull-out would be steep until they could fell a few trees. But it was possible, and the sand seemed firm and pebbly. This, then, would be "Palm Beach."

Should they carry in firearms? It was a delicate question. They knew that the first shot fired would scuttle the entire project. Yet it would be criminally naïve to go in totally unarmed.

It was claimed that no one carrying a gun was ever attacked; the Aucas apparently had a healthy regard for this strange weapon. "The handier the revolver," Nate argued, "the less chance of a hostile encounter." The team finally agreed to take guns along—but keep them out of sight, use them only in direst emergency, and then only to frighten the savages if attacked.

They planned to allow five days for the beachhead effort. If it failed in that time they could leave by air, barring floods, in which case a crew of Quechuas could come down-river for them in canoes. They would bring in a prefabricated tree-house and stock it with food for two weeks. This would allow a few days' margin if a state of siege developed.

Another thing: they needed a fifth man. Once the beachhead was established, one should guard the tree-house at all times, two should patrol the beach, another should attend to the supplies and cooking, with Nate on whatever in-and-out flight duty was required.

Marj Saint produced a list of available missionaries in the area. The team pored over it. Nate's finger ran down the list, stopped at the name of Roger Youderian, of the Gospel Missionary Union. "What about Roj?" he asked.

Raised on a Montana ranch, former paratrooper, a veteran of the Battle of the Bulge, later chosen as a member of General Eisenhower's honor guard, Roger Youderian was a man who would not duck danger in any form. He had not ducked it in Ecuador. No emergency that arose—and there had been a lot of them at Macuma, his mission post deep in the domain of the head-hunting Jivaros—had ever been too perilous or too difficult for him to meet with resolution and quiet strength.

The team recalled a dozen exploits of Roger's. One had happened only a few months before when, after calling Shell Mera for penicillin, he had tramped two days through the jungle to an outstation called Paki where an epidemic threatened the Jivaros, hacked out an airstrip for Nate to land, seized the medicine from the plane before its wheels had scarcely stopped rolling—and halted the epidemic in its tracks.

And there was the time a Jivaro worker, helping clear a new airstrip, had been struck by a falling tree. Roger, 18 miles away, had heard the news, called Nate for help at 10 A.M., and set out on foot to cover these 18 tortuous miles by 4 o'clock, when he had requested the plane to be ready to bring the Indian out.

Said Nate, "When I got over the narrow cut in the matted green that was the airstrip, there was Roj, signaling OK on the strip's condition. Haggard, his shirt in shreds, scratched and bruised, he helped me load the mangled Jivaro into the plane—and we got him to Shell just in time for the doctor there to save his life."

"We could use a fellow like that," said Jim Elliot, "*if* he'll come."

The "if" was redundant. When invited, Roger grinned cheerfully and welcomed the opportunity to share in the venture.

On Monday, January 2, the team members and their wives gathered at Arajuno. All day they worked making ready for the beachhead, preparing food, packing equipment. Before they were through, the mission grounds looked like a D-day staging area.

At nightfall, wives and husbands withdrew in couples to be alone together. Wrapped in the jungle fastness of the isolated station, they frankly faced the risks, soberly discussed their futures and what the morrow might bring.

Did the young wives intuitively sense what lay ahead? That this might be their last night together? Perhaps. In any case, they were ready.

To Roger, Barbara Youderian whispered, "Remember the verse we chose as ours when we started life together? 'Being confident of this very thing, that he which hath begun a good work in you will perform it until the day of Jesus Christ.' Hold our verse close to your heart, Roj!"

Betty Elliot told her husband, "I've been privileged above any woman in having such a husband, Jim. I shall thank God always for the two years of perfect happiness He has granted us. If there is to be no more, what more fitting way is there to die—at the height of your manhood, with your dearest friends, and in the attempt to reach the people so near to your heart for so long."

Olive Fleming, her head on Pete's shoulder, expressed her faith in a prayer-verse loved by them both:

I am the Lord's—yet teach me all it meaneth,
All it involves of love and loyalty,
Of holy service, absolute surrender
And unreserved obedience to Thee.

"When the Lord gave us the desire to reach unreached Indians," Marilou McCully reminded Ed, "the first place he laid on our hearts was Arajuno, right here where no missionary ever lived before us. We were confident of that leading, Ed. Now the Lord has put the Aucas on our hearts too. With that same confidence we can follow His leading now—together."

Of the five wives, only Marjorie Saint was not at Arajuno that night. Hers was the duty to man the "radio central" at Shell Mera. But between her and Nate no further covenant was necessary. Days before, she'd said: "Nate, you've always told me that every believer should be willing to give his all for Christ—even his life, if God's mysterious purposes required it. During all these years, we've faced many dangers together—for Him. We are in God's will and care."

As for the men, they had already faced up to the dangers ahead. Nate spoke for all when he told his wife, "There is no doubt in my mind that we should go ahead. The stakes warrant it."

Thus, after the most careful preparation, and in complete unity and magnificent dedication, Operation Auca had come to its D-day.

Next morning the young couples held a brief prayer service. And, just before leaving, they sang together the hymn which became the theme song for Operation Auca:

We rest on Thee, our Shield
and our Defender!
Thine is the battle, Thine shall
be the praise;
When passing through the gates
of pearly splendor,
Victors, we rest with Thee,
through endless days.

At 8:02, only two minutes behind schedule, Nate lifted the Piper into the air. A few minutes later, after hazardous landing and equally hazardous take-off from the beachhead sand, he had left Ed McCully (who had drawn straws for the privilege) as the first occupant of Palm Beach. Then he returned to Arajuno for another load. Altogether he made five trips to the beachhead that day, ferrying in the men and supplies. There was not time for a sixth, so Peter Fleming had to remain at the mission overnight.

Next morning, Wednesday, when Nate and Pete flew to the beachhead, they circled over Terminal City on the way and, using the loud-speaker, invited the Aucas to visit their camp. The Aucas waved in a friendly manner and seemed to understand. An hour later, when they again circled over the village to repeat the invitation, Nate saw that all the men had disappeared. Were the Aucas already on their way?

At the beach, where the tree-house had now been set up and routine organized, the missionaries made every possible gesture of friendliness. They mounted a model airplane on a pole, placed a gift machete at the edge of the jungle, and at intervals throughout the day marched up and down the beach shouting Auca phrases of welcome.

But no Auca showed up. From the jungle came only strange bird calls and the protesting squawk of parrots.

"Perhaps they'll come tomorrow," Pete said. And remembering the absence of men from the village, he added, "It's plain that the Aucas are looking for us somewhere."

Thursday, however, was equally unrewarding: flights over Terminal City still revealed no male Aucas; the calls into the jungle still brought no response. Yet the gift machete left out the night before was gone, and the men felt sure that, from behind that thick jungle curtain, "we are being watched."

Slowly the day passed, with intervals of fishing and swimming, reading, making notes. By 4:30 that afternoon all agreed that the Aucas probably were not coming that day. Yet they were determined to "sweat it out" until the savages could locate their camp and show themselves.

That evening Nate and Pete went back to Arajuno to sleep, since the tree-house was uncomfortably crowded for five people. On their way they flew over the Auca settlement. As they spiraled down, an Auca climbed up on one of the platforms, knelt toward the direction of the camp site, pointed with both hands. It was an encouraging sign, and that night Nate wrote in his diary: "We find we have a friendlier feeling for these fellows all the time. We must not let that lead us to carelessness. It is no small thing to try to bridge between the 20th century and the Stone Age. God help us to take care. . . . *But may we see them soon!*"

See them soon they did. The long-awaited contact occurred the next morning, Friday, January 6.

Confident now that a delegation of some sort was on its

way, the team had arisen early to begin the verbal bombard-
ments of the jungle. At midmorning Ed McCully was on one
end of the beach, Jim Elliot on the other, with Roger Youderian, Nate and Pete in between—all taking turns shouting
phrases and waving gifts.

Suddenly, from directly across the river, a strong mascu-
line voice boomed out, and immediately three Aucas stepped
out in the open. They were a man and two women—one
about 30 years of age, the other a well-formed girl of about
16. They were naked except for G-strings about the waist
and large wooden plugs in distended ear lobes.

The missionaries, temporarily struck dumb by the surprise
appearance, finally managed to shout simultaneously, *"Pui-
nani!"*—Auca for "Welcome."

The Auca man replied with a verbal flood, pointing frequently to the girl. His language was unintelligible, but not
his gestures. "He's offering the girl for trade," exclaimed
Pete, "or maybe as a gift."

Jim Elliot yelled, "I don't know what they've come for.
But they've come—and that's enough for me!" He yanked
off his outer clothes and began wading across the shallow
river.

At Jim's impulsive plunge, the Aucas shrank back a trifle
toward the jungle. But as he approached them, hands extended, the girl edged forward and stepped off a log into the
water. The man and the other woman followed slowly. Jim
seized their hands and led them across.

With broad smiles, many *puinanis* and much reference
to their phrase books, the five conveyed that their visitors
had "come well" and need not be afraid. The Aucas' uneasi-
ness fell from them, and they began jabbering happily to

themselves and the men, "seemingly with little idea that we didn't understand them."

Roger brought out some paring knives, which they accepted with cries of delight. Nate presented a machete and the model airplane. The others, suddenly remembering the guns in the cook shack and tree-house, went back to hide the weapons beneath their duffel. They dug out cameras and shot dozens of photos, while the women looked through a copy of *Time* magazine and the man was being doused with insecticide to demonstrate civilization's way of dealing with the swarming insects.

Presently the girl drifted over toward the Piper, rubbing her body against the fabric and imitating with her hands the plane's movement. The Auca man followed. He was completely unafraid and self-possessed—but obviously curious to know more about the "big bird." The missionaries promptly named him "George," and the girl "Delilah."

By sign language George made it plain he wanted a ride in the Piper. Finally Nate agreed, and the Auca eagerly climbed in. Nate taxied down the strip and took off, with George shouting all the way. Suddenly Nate realized his opportunity to use his passenger for propaganda, and headed for Terminal City. George chortled with delight, leaned out to wave and yell at his fellow villagers, whose mouths fell open at sight of him in the plane.

Back on the beach, the missionaries demonstrated for their guests such modern marvels as rubber bands, balloons, a yo-yo; served them lemonade and hamburger with mustard. Then they tried to get across the idea that an invitation to visit the Auca village would not be scorned. For this notion George displayed no enthusiasm.

"Why is it he's so reluctant whenever we broach the subject?" one of the five demanded. Another replied, "Maybe he lacks the authority to invite us on his own."

As the day wore on, Delilah showed signs of impatience. Once when Jim Elliot left the group to go to the tree-house she leapt up and followed. She seemed downcast when he turned and rejoined the others.

The rest of the day was spent in rampant friendliness. When the Aucas showed signs of wanting to spend the night on the beach, the missionaries hospitably offered them a small beach shack they had constructed, motioning that it was theirs to occupy if they wished.

Suddenly Delilah wheeled and walked off down the beach. George called to her, but she kept going. He followed her into the forest, and the older woman left later.

When Nate and Pete got back to Arajuno that night, they held the waiting wives agog with an account of the day's adventures. They were in high spirits. Months of prayerful preparation and years of dreaming had brought their reward. The three days' nerve-racking vigil on Palm Beach had paid off. For today they had accomplished what no white men had ever accomplished before them: they had stood face to face with the fearsome Aucas—and on friendly terms.

The next day, Saturday, was anticlimactic. They waited hopefully, expecting the Aucas to return momentarily with an invitation to their village. But none came.

During the day Nate made three calls over Terminal City. On the first he was puzzled to see the women and children run for cover. Only two men appeared, and they seemed frightened. But when he called over the loud-speaker, "Come . . . come . . . come!" and threw out gifts of a blanket, a pot and a pair of nylon shorts, "they seemed relieved."

On the second trip over, the Aucas manifested less fear. This time there were several men in the clearing—"George" among them. An old man pointed toward Palm Beach "and seemed friendly, though not exuberant."

On the third flight all evidence of fear seemed to have vanished. Nate reported, "I got some good smiles from 'George' and another young man who, one can imagine, probably aspires to ride in the plane."

That night, again at Arajuno, Nate tossed sleeplessly, in hindsight thinking of devices they might have used to detain their Friday visitors. But Sunday morning before taking off he confided to Pete, "I have a hunch that things will happen today."

He and Pete climbed into the Piper at 8:45. Pete called to the wives: "Good-by, girls, pray for us—for I believe today's the day."

Back at Palm Beach, they found that Ed, Jim and Roger also had spent a restless night. They, too, sensed somehow that "today things will happen."

When nothing had happened by midmorning, Nate took off to scout the situation. Over the Auca settlement, he again saw only a handful of women and children—no men.

On the way back, however, he suddenly spotted figures moving along a river beach. He came down for a closer look, counted ten Auca men. They were heading toward the Curaray.

"I believe they're coming, fellows!" Nate shouted before his wheels had stopped rolling. The four set up a yell. They had a brief song and prayer service, ate a quick lunch and fell to work arranging the beach and shack for company.

Promptly at 12:35 P.M., their prearranged radio-contact time, Nate transmitted the tidings to the wives. Breathlessly, and still using their code words, he told of spotting "a commission of ten" on the way from Terminal City, adding, "Looks like they'll be here for an early-afternoon service. Pray for us. This *is* the day! Will contact you next at 4:35."

The contact was never made. Before 4:35 that afternoon all five had fallen beneath the lances and machetes of the Aucas, their lifeblood mingling with the soft sand and muddy waters of the Curaray.

Along the Curaray all was quiet. Yet hovering over the scene were a host of unanswered questions. When did it happen? The only clue was Nate Saint's damaged wrist watch, found on his spear-pierced body days later. It had stopped at 3:12.

Had there been a struggle? Later examinations of the beach and the tree-house offered no such evidence. Had the ten Aucas first feigned friendliness, then turned on their unwary victims? It would seem so, for all were slain on the beach—indicating that even the one set to cover any approach from the tree-house had come down.

The little yellow Piper stood forlornly on the beach, pierced by several spears, its yellow fabric stripped—as though the Indians, regarding the plane as some evil bird, had felt they must kill it too.

But even more mysterious than what happened is: Why? Why did the savages, who had shown such cordiality during the gift exchanges, and again two days before in face-to-face encounter, revert to type? Had "George" returned to the

village with accounts of that friendliness, with perhaps urgings to pursue it—only to be overruled by the headmen of
the village whose ingrained fear of strangers had not yet
been quite conquered? Or had the Aucas been affronted
by the missionaries' rejection of Delilah—in the form she had
obviously been offered—and come to avenge the insult?

One can only speculate. The questions remain.

Back at the mission stations that Sunday afternoon the
wives waited eagerly for the 4:35 contact. When it didn't
come, they concluded that perhaps the men were busy
entertaining the Aucas, or maybe having trouble with their
transmitter. Then, at Shell Mera, Marj tried calling. No
answer.

The hours dragged by. The wives remained glued to their
radios. Said Marj Saint wistfully, "This is the first time since
Nate started jungle flying in '48 that we've been out of contact for even an hour."

The suspense was the sharper because most of their missionary friends in the network were unaware that Operation Auca was in progress. Should they call for help, and
thereby divulge the secret? They decided to wait until they
were sure something serious had happened.

Early Monday morning Johnny Keenan, Nate's team-
mate at Shell Mera, who had been in on the operation from
the beginning, took off in his Piper for Palm Beach. Presently he radioed that Nate's plane seemed to be stripped of
its fabric, and that there was no sign of the men. The wives,
quickly flown to Shell Mera from their isolated stations,
conferred with heavy hearts. Something, plainly, had gone
terribly wrong. By midmorning they'd made their decision:

they would appeal for help. Marj relayed the facts to radio station HCJB at Quito, known as "The Voice of the Andes," which then put the news on the air.

Search operations were begun at once. A detachment of Ecuadorian soldiers, missionaries and Quechua Indians was dispatched to the spot; planes and a helicopter were sent over. But the searchers could report only tragedy—a rifled camp, a stripped and broken plane, spear-pierced bodies floating in the river. Four of the bodies were recovered. Ed McCully's, brutally mutilated by a machete slash, was seen and identified by a party of Quechua Indians who had come down the river ahead of the search party; but it disappeared beneath the muddy waters, and was never found.

That afternoon the wives were informed of the day's grim discoveries. Observers were moved at the quiet fortitude with which they received the news. "We expected hysteria," one reporter commented. "We are seeing instead an eloquent testimony to the power and beauty of the faith for which these men gave their lives."

At the request of the women, their husbands' bodies remained at the site and were buried in a common grave dug beneath the tree-house. One said quietly: "There they lived for six wonderful days. There they preached, by word and action, the gospel of God's salvation for all—even Aucas. There they should rest until the Resurrection."

The day after the burial, the five women asked to be flown over Palm Beach. From the plane, looking down through tears at the beach, they saw the rough mound beneath the tree-house. "It's the most beautiful little cemetery in the world," murmured Marj Saint.

While the plane circled over the site, they read from II Corinthians 5, then knelt together on the corrugated floor of the plane, commending their loved ones to God, pledging in prayer that "we too may be faithful in all that God asks of us."

Someone started singing the "theme song" they had sung with the men on that last breakfast together. The others picked up the refrain:

> *We rest on Thee, our Shield*
> *and our Defender!*
> *Thine is the battle, Thine shall*
> *be the praise;*
> *When passing through the gates*
> *of pearly splendor,*
> *Victors, we rest with Thee,*
> *through endles days.*

And as the C-47 began its slow upward circle away from the site, they stared down at the receding beach, saying no more, each wrapped in her own thoughts, thinking not of themselves but of their men. One opened her Bible to read, "When thou passest through the waters, I will be with thee; and through the rivers, they shall not overflow thee . . ." From her purse Betty Elliot took out a frayed piece of paper; it was a little poem Jim had written five years before:

> *The tide of night has washed away*
> *The littered shore of yesterday,*
> *And I discover at the dawn*
> *A fresh-swept beach to walk upon.*

During that harrowing week the big rambling mission house at Shell Mera, which Nate and Marj had built with their own hands, swarmed with guests. They were participants in the search and rescue operation, armed forces personnel, mechanics servicing the planes, press and radio correspondents, missionaries come in from distant stations to do what they could.

At first the wives were overwhelmed by the public concern that flowed over and around them. For the first time, their humble doings in this remote corner of earth were in the blazing light of publicity. But they quickly adjusted, mercifully were kept busy caring for their children, feeding and bedding down the scores of guests coming and going.

A puzzled U.S. airman watched them a while, then commented, "There's a—well, a sort of radiance about those women that gets you. How do they do it?" His companion drew him to the door of the temporarily evacuated living-room. He pointed to one of the widows at the piano; thinking she was alone, Barbara Youderian was running her hands over the keys, softly singing. The airman strained his ears, caught the words: "Were the whole realm of nature mine, that were an offering far too small. Love so amazing, so divine, demands my soul, my life, my all."

On February 16 Dr. José Maria Velasco Ibarra, President of Ecuador, posthumously awarded the slain missionaries the "Order of Merit in the Rank of Commander" for "sacrificial service in behalf of the inhabitants of the eastern jungles"—the highest recognition ever given Protestants in Ecuador. And in the United States a fund was started to provide emergency aid for the five wives and education for their nine children. Money flowed in, and within a few weeks an impressive sum was subscribed—most of it in small bills.

The death of the five did not end Operation Auca. Within three weeks Johnny Keenan, Nate's companion pilot at Shell Mera, was continuing the flights and gift drops over the settlement. Meanwhile, mission groups back in the United States were processing a score of applications from fliers anxious to take Nate Saint's place. The effort to reach the Aucas, far from being abandoned, now promised to be intensified.

The weeks immediately following the tragedy brought astonishing response. Evidence quickly accumulated to prove that the drama on the Curaray was shaking the Christian Church back in the United States as it had not been shaken in a generation. From widely spread colleges more than 1000 students volunteered to enter the foreign-mission field. Mission boards announced new plans to reach not only Aucas but others of the yet-to-be-contacted tribes—such as those in New Guinea, the Philippines, Indo-China, the Amazon Valley, north central Africa.

A news commentator observed, "I'm no missionary, but for years I have been watching them and this I know: The Aucas are marked men—marked not for extinction but for conversion. As such, they haven't a chance. Missionaries, especially those touched by martyrdom, are hard to stop. The blood of martyrs seems still to be the seed of the Church!"

Even more astonishing were the reactions at the mission stations the men had served. Attendance at schools and church services reached record levels. From Shandia, Betty

Elliot reported that within a few weeks more Indians had come into the Church than in many months before the five died. One of the converts had turned into an evangelist of exceptional talents—"a long step toward Jim's greatest desire, namely that spiritual leadership here would one day devolve wholly upon the Indians themselves."

Two Christian Quechuas at Arajuno, formerly as fearful of their "neighbors" as the rest of the Quechua tribe, volunteered to devote their lives to converting the Aucas. From Macuma, Barbara Youderian reported that when Roger's sacrifice became known to the Jivaros, ten stepped forth to say they loved their Lord enough to die for Him in like manner. One Jivaro, whose father had been a witch-doctor responsible for many raids on a rival tribe, volunteered to go at once to the enemy with a message of Christian good will. He did so, bringing the first peace between the tribes in years.

To the wives, such results, so much greater than they or their husbands had dared dream, were a revelation of God's larger design.

At Shell Mera, Marj Saint said humbly: "His plan seems to have reached much farther than the Aucas—for whom alone the fellows were willing to die. That He should use this to His greater glory is none of our doing.

"But isn't that His way," she added: "using the small things to confound the mighty?"

In that simple attitude and expression is summed up the dauntless faith that has moved all missionaries, crowned all martyrs, since their Master first said, "Go ye . . . for lo, I am with you alway, even unto the end."